Breaking the Barriers

A survey of managers' attitudes to age and employment

James Arrowsmith
& Ann McGoldrick

First published 1996

The Institute of Management
2 Savoy Court
Strand
London
WC2R 0EZ

British Library Cataloguing in Publication Data

A CIP catalogue record for this report is available from the British Library

ISBN 0-85946-255-2

Contents

Key Findings

- Age discrimination can be experienced by young and old alike. However, the ages of 40 and 50 are the key markers when age can become more of an acute consideration.
- More than four in ten respondents believe that women experience age discrimination at earlier ages than men.
- There is a clear recognition of a relationship between age and a range of important employment characteristics. Older workers, for example, may be seen as more reliable, committed and providing a better quality of work but are less flexible, energetic, ambitious and able to learn.
- Age discrimination is more likely in recruitment and redundancy rather than internal training or promotion. Over half the respondents believe that older people have a lower chance of being recruited and a higher chance of experiencing redundancy in their organisation solely due to their age.
- Around four in ten respondents also believe that older employees in their organisation may face disadvantage concerning training or promotion.
- Over half the respondents (55 per cent) have used age as a criterion in subordinate recruitment and selection. Over a quarter (29 per cent) have used age when judging a promotion, 25 per cent in relation to training and nearly a third (32 per cent) when considering a redundancy or dismissal situation. Fifty per cent of respondents believe that age can be a legitimate consideration in recruitment and selection decision-making.
- Nearly a third of respondents (32 per cent) report the formal use of age in recruitment and selection by their organisation. A majority (53 per cent) believe that age is extensively used on an informal basis.

- Age barriers are more likely to be found in larger organisations and especially where efforts are being made to reduce employee numbers. Managers in SMEs are more positive about the future recruitment of older workers.

- The most important reasons for age barriers in recruitment relate to the use of age as a convenient filter device to manage a large pool of applications. Other important reasons include the operation of career and succession planning processes and the perceived need for recruits to fit an existing team profile.

- Promotion opportunities for managers of all ages appear to be diminishing as a result of restructuring and delayering. Taken together with the effect of increasingly early retirement this could serve to lower the developmental age ceiling so that age barriers in promotion are experienced at earlier ages.

- Within the last five years, nearly seven in ten (67 per cent) of respondent organisations had made efforts to reduce the size of the workforce. This is especially the case for larger organisations and this figure rises to over eight in ten for both public sector organisations and public limited companies.

- Nearly six in ten respondents in these downsizing organisations (58 per cent) report that efforts had focused on older employees. This is again especially true for the large organisations and may be facilitated by occupational pension schemes.

- Managers recognise a number of advantages associated with age-related redundancy and early retirement schemes but they are also aware of the potential costs involved in the loss of skilled and experienced personnel. Eight out of ten respondents believe that their organisation should not focus on older employees as a means of reducing headcount.

- A majority of respondents favour legislation aimed at age discrimination. Nearly seven in ten per cent support legislation to restrict the use of age in job advertisements and 65 per cent are in favour of comprehensive employment protection legislation similar to that for race and sex issues in employment. This feeling is consistent across all age groups.

- The case for legislation is made on the grounds of both individual fairness and organisational efficiency. Some respondents feel however that it may be unnecessary, ineffective and even counter-productive bureaucratic interference in managerial decision-making.

- Written equal opportunity policies are reported by 63 per cent of respondents and these are especially likely in the large and public sector organisations. A reference to age is included in only a third (34 per cent) of these formal policies.

- Respondents hold a very positive view of equal opportunity activity in the organisation. Nine out of ten see it as an important moral issue, 73 per cent believe it to be an important business issue and 62 per cent recognise it to be a mainstream managerial activity.

- A large majority of respondents (85 per cent) believe that employers *should* treat age as an equal opportunity issue. A similar figure believe that this should be of at least equal importance to the more traditional areas of race, sex and disability.

Introduction

Age is one of the most commonly used means of social classification. It is used both formally and informally, by other individuals and by all manner of institutions, to group and to categorise people.

In employment terms, this process can be conducted with little real regard to individual skills, characteristics and abilities. Young and older workers alike may experience disadvantage, or preference, simply due to their age. Yet understanding of the patterns or reasons for the use of age in employment decision making remains limited.

In recent years a number of studies have been undertaken, although these have tended to focus on personnel/human resource management samples and/or have used a relatively small sample framework. Empirical work has suggested, for example, that older workers in particular may experience employment disadvantage due to age[1,2], although recruitment obstacles may really begin in the early to mid thirties[3]. Older workers may also be seen as a 'last resort' option by both public and private sector employers[4,5]. This could relate to managerial stereotypes held of older workers[6], although a number of pragmatic and institutional reasons may also be of importance.

This research was designed to provide evidence on a wider set of key issues from a large sample of practising managers. These respondents are in a position to report on recent and anticipated developments from a range of different organisations as they emerge from recession into a still uncertain world. Managers were asked, where appropriate, for their personal views and experiences, in addition to reporting on organisational policy and practice.

The research was undertaken against the background of efforts made by the Government to persuade organisations not to discriminate on the basis of age. Awareness of these issues has greatly increased in recent years. The Government, for example, has established an Advisory Committee on the subject of age discrimination and has begun a series of campaigns ('Getting On') to promote the skills and abilities of the neglected older worker resource. Employers themselves are also beginning to take this on board and an Employers' Forum on Age is presently in the process of being established. The personnel profession has adopted a Statement on Age and Employment and the house journal "People Management" has had a policy since January 1996 not to accept recruitment advertising containing references to age. The issue of age discrimination is also regularly taken up in Parliament although the most recent Private Member's Bill did not succeed at its Second Reading in February 1996.

The research for this project was undertaken in two stages. In May 1995, a pilot questionnaire was distributed to 1000 members of the Institute of Management, attracting a response rate of 36 per cent. The second stage of the project was conducted in September 1995, when the views of nearly 1700 managers were obtained through a postal questionnaire sent to a random sample of 5000 IM members (a response rate of 33 per cent).

The questionnaire is reproduced as Appendix 1. A seven-point Likert scale was adopted in order to better approximate to continuity for the purposes of the various statistical tests. Variables within the tables in the text are ordered according to the mean score where appropriate except for Table 7 (see note 11). The results are discussed in a non-technical fashion.

In addition to completing pre-coded questions, respondents were invited to offer written comments - on a non-attributable basis - on specific questions or in general. These comments were captured and are used throughout the text to illustrate the statistical findings.

The report is organised into three principal sections. The first examines the possibility of a perceived association between age and a number of work characteristics. This is explored at both a general level, in order to examine the potential and nature of any managerial age stereotyping, and specifically and comparatively in relation to the respondent's own workplace. The second examines the extent, patterns and reasons for the use of age in organisational entry, development, and exit practices. The third focuses on managerial attitudes to age as an equality of opportunity issue and to the prospect of legislation concerning age discrimination.

Profile of Respondents

Base: All respondents	%
Sex	
Male	94
Female	6
Age	
Under 30	1
30 - 39	11
40 - 49	41
50 - 59	39
Over 59	8
Location by region	
Northern Ireland	2
Scotland	8
North East	8
North West	8
Wales	4
West Midlands	10
East Midlands	8
East Anglia	7
South West	10
South East	21
London	15
Management level	
Board/chief executive	27
Senior management	37
Middle management	24
Junior management	5
Supervisory management	3
Other	5

Management function	
General management	34
Production/engineering	9
Marketing/sales	9
Consultancy	8
Finance	6
Administration	6
Computing/IT	4
Personnel/HR/IR	3
Education	3
Management services	2
R&D/design	2
Training	2
Purchasing/contracting	2
Distribution	1
Other	10
Type of organisation	
Public sector	23
Public limited company	22
Private limited company	34
Voluntary sector	2
Owner managed/partnership	13
Other	5
Activity of organisation	
Manufacturing/processing	17
Professional/consultancy/business services	16
Education/training	10
Public administration/local government	9
Engineering	7
Banking/insurance/finance	5
Health services	4
Construction	4
Energy/water supply	4
Other services	3
Communications	3
Emergency/armed services	3
Retail/wholesale	3
Distribution/transport	3
Hotel/catering/leisure	2
Other	10

Profile	%
Number of employees	
1 - 6	12
7 - 24	9
25 - 99	12
100 - 499	19
500 - 999	7
1000 - 4999	17
Over 5000	23
Workforce characteristics (site of work)	
Mostly male	47
Mostly female	14
Equally divided	39
Mostly young	18
Mostly mature	33
Equally divided	49
Employee relations	
Separate personnel/HR section	62
Trade union recognition	49
Company pension scheme	80
Note: Percentages may not total 100 due to rounding	

Table 1: Profile of respondents

The profile is representative of IM membership. Respondents are overwhelmingly male and the majority are aged over 40. Most describe themselves as engaged in senior or middle management roles and a third classify their job as having cross-functional general management responsibilities.

One in five work in organisations with fewer than twenty five employees; twice this number work in organisations with one thousand or more employees. A quarter work in the manufacturing or engineering industries and 23 per cent are employed in the public sector. Over a third of respondents live and work in London and the South East.

1. Attitudes to Ageing and Work

Managerial attitudes regarding the possibility of an association between age and a range of important employment characteristics were explored at both the general and organisational levels. Managers were asked in the first instance, however, to specify how they might define an older employee.

1.1 Who is an'Older Employee'?

Managers were invited to suggest an (uncoded) age for defining an older employee in their organisation. The range of responses, referring both to male and female employees, is shown in Table 2.

Base: All respondents		
Age in years	**For men %**	**For women %**
Under 40	2	8
40 - 44	11	17
45 - 49	15	16
50 - 54	35	34
55 - 59	21	15
60 +	16	10
Mean	51	48

Table 2: Definition of a male and female older employee

The results support earlier research that age might begin to be a consideration around the age of forty, intensifying up to the age of 50[9]. The average age given is 51 for male employees and 48 for female employees, suggesting that women may be perceived to be 'older workers' at earlier ages than for men. Over four in ten respondents, for example, place the defining female age below fifty whereas this applies for men in only 28 per cent of cases. Overall, 42 per cent of respondents stated a younger female than male age.

This difference tends to be more pronounced where female employees are in a minority or mixed sex workforce. It may be the case that sex and age issues inter-relate to the disadvantage of women: women may fall behind for example if they leave the labour force for family reasons and so be relatively older at each stage in the organisational timetable. It must also be remembered, however, that more than nine out of ten respondents are men.

That age is essentially relative is borne out by the strong positive correlation between the definition of an 'older employee' and the respondents' own age. Younger managers tend to define the older worker at earlier ages than do older respondents. The stated ages also tend to be younger for those in larger organisations, one possible effect of the widespread use of early retirement and age-related redundancy by such firms.

1.2 Ageing and Employment in General

Respondents were then asked to indicate whether and how they might perceive certain characteristics to display a tendency to increase with age, others to decrease and others to remain fairly stable. Some of the main results are shown in Figure 1 (the full results are presented in Appendix 2).

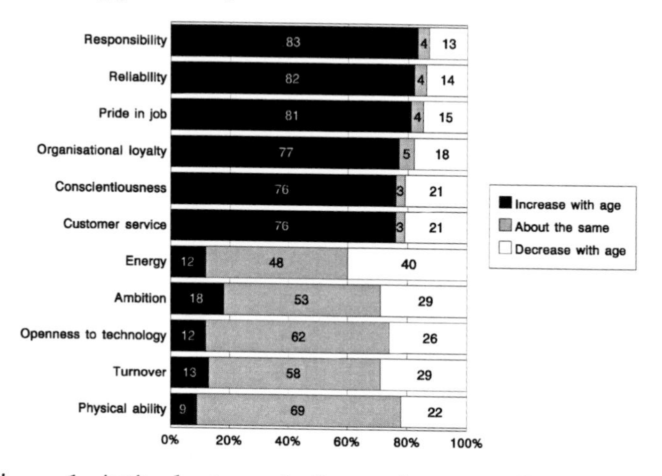

Figure 1: Attitudes towards the employment effects of ageing

The results show that managers have a strong view of the potential relationship between age and a range of important employment characteristics. Respondents observe a clear pattern in that some characteristics are seen to become more pronounced with age whereas others have a tendency to decrease, with either positive or negative implications for the organisation.

Firstly, many characteristics are seen to increase with age. Around three quarters of respondents would recognise increases in reliability, responsibility, loyalty to the organisation, pride in the job, conscientiousness, customer service, skills, confidence, and a commitment to quality. Similarly, around two thirds would assert an increase in work quality and one half might believe that older workers are more efficient, enjoy more job satisfaction, cope better under pressure and have a better ability to work in teams and under authority. A majority of respondents also believe, however, that wage and pension costs increase with age.

Respondents are divided over the second group of characteristics with many observing an increase with age and others noting stability. These relate in positive terms to employee motivation and productivity, and more negatively to long-term absence and benefits and insurance costs. For the third group of characteristics respondents are divided three ways, with many stating perceived increases with age, others a decrease and other managers observing stability. These relate to work speed and potential, sickness, and interest in training.

Respondents tend to note a decrease with age or general stability in relation to flexibility, 'trainability', energy and short term absence. Most respondents believe that the incidence of accidents occur independently of individual age.

Finally, respondents believe that ambition, physical ability and openess to technology fall with age, along with rates of employee turnover.

Accordingly, on the whole attitudes appear to be positive but with some important qualifications. Managers may be convinced, for example, that reliability, loyalty, service and quality of work increase with age and that turnover and short-term absence may be likely to reduce. On the other hand, flexibility, energy, ambition and openness to technology may be seen to diminish with age, whereas some employment costs may be higher. These sets of attitudes might be a factor in defining jobs as suitable to older - or younger - employees:

> *"I tend to recruit older workers for routine jobs as they are much more stable".*

> *"I would always prefer older people in a customer contact role".*

These general level perceptions tend not to vary substantially on the whole according to personal or organisational characteristics, except for respondent age. Although the overall patterns can still be observed, older respondents tend to hold the 'positive' views more strongly and the 'negative' views relatively more weakly than do the younger managers. This could have important implications where junior managers hold responsibilities for routine recruitment and selection, in that younger managers tend to have a more negative overall perception of older workers.

A factor analysis (principal components) was performed which reduces the variables listed in Appendix 2 into seven key dimensions (explained variance = 58 per cent).

An examination of these results serves to clarify how managers view the relationship between age and work. The factors can be labelled as measures of:

- job commitment
- change orientation
- work pace
- maturity
- stability
- primary and secondary costs

This identifies the principal sources of ambivalence in managerial attitudes and may help to explain why older (and younger) people may be seen as particularly suitable for some jobs but not for others.

Older workers, for example, may be viewed as generally more committed to the job and to the organisation. This can be translated in turn into improved efficiency and quality of work. However, they may be seen as less interested in, and less able to cope with, change in the workplace. Older workers may also be viewed as less able to maintain a demanding pace of work, especially if the job involves any real physical requirements.

Older workers may, however, be viewed as better able personally to cope under pressure and this 'maturity' may also be expressed in terms of more effective relationships in the workplace with peers and superiors.

They may also be seen as more stable employees, especially in terms of absenteeism and retention. Older workers may be viewed, however, as generally more expensive to employ, both in terms of direct (pay and pensions) and secondary costs (insurance and other benefits).

Accordingly, managers may view older people as less suitable, for example, for jobs requiring a sustained level of heavy or fast paced work; or for rapidly changing jobs and those requiring a high training component. In contrast, they may be viewed positively for jobs which involve team-working or customer contact, especially if the job does not require a close degree of supervision.

1.3 Older Workers in the Organisation

Respondents were then asked to compare directly older workers with other employees in the workforce with which they are most familiar. The results show that even when basing answers specifically on their experience in the workplace, a similar pattern of attitudes can be detected. Figure 2 shows that managers might recognise a better quality of work from the older employees, but believe that they may be less open to technology or able to learn. This could serve to threaten the position of older workers in conditions of change. Significantly, however, between approximately a third and a half of respondents for each aspect of employment believe that no overall difference between the older workers and others can be detected.

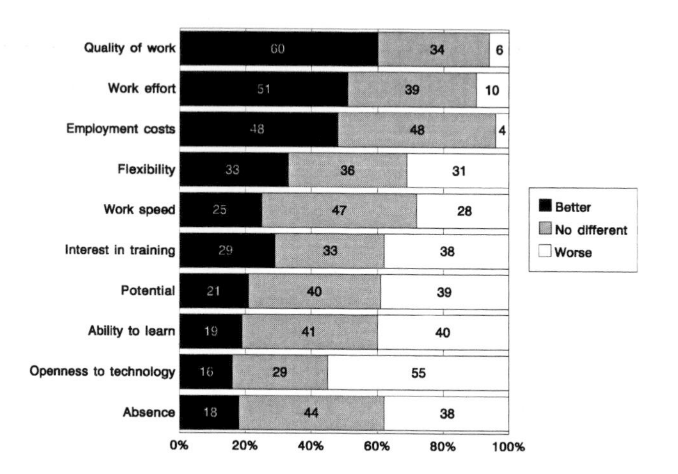

Figure 2: Attitudes at the specific level - comparing older workers to others

Almost half of the managers surveyed believe that older workers are more costly to employ in their organisation. Analyses indicate that age-related increases in employment costs tend to be associated with the larger organisations, particularly in the public sector. Costs are reported to increase significantly in the education sector and also in banking and finance; communications and the utilities. The relationship is less evident within construction, health, transport, hotel and catering and retailing. The former industries may be characterised as historically long service employers operating sophisticated internal labour markets, often using seniority-based systems of pay and promotion and with extensive occupational pension coverage. The decline in the use of seniority systems, whereby employee pay and benefits may be related to age (directly or indirectly through service enhancements), in all but the education sector might imply that cost concerns could become less of a problem for older worker employment in the future.

When directly comparing attitudes to age and employment firstly in general and secondly in the workplace we find that the overall results are broadly similar. In some cases (for example, concerning employment flexibility) managerial reservations may be less pronounced for older workers within the organisation than for older workers in general. This suggests that older employees with whom respondents are familiar may be seen as more capable than older workers overall on these issues. However, the similarity between attitudes at the general and the specific levels could also suggest that the nature of these generalisations (or stereotypes) may be more than merely subjectively formed and prejudicial perceptions. It could be that these stereotypes are constructed at least in part from actual employment experience. If so, then it could be argued that there may be a legitimate (albeit secondary) role for using age stereotypes as a tool to assist efficient decision-making, especially in recruitment and selection where objective and individual-centred criteria are less easy to apply.

As at the general level, younger managers tend to have a less positive set of views concerning the employment capabilities of older people in the workplace. It also emerges that, when we allow for the direct association between age and respondent job level in the statistical analysis, attitudes regarding the relative performance of older employees become less positive with increasing managerial seniority.

The explanation for this relationship could be that managers were asked to respond on the basis of the workforce with which they had the highest degree of familiarity and this would most likely to relate to peers and/or close subordinates. Accordingly, this relationship between managerial level and attitudes could suggest that older employees may be viewed as more effective relative to colleagues in the less senior posts.

1.4 *Qualifying Managerial Views I: 'It Depends on the Job'*

Some of the categories used are not unambiguous and much depends on the nature of the job in question. Personal ambition, for example, might be viewed as a negative characteristic if it leads to reduced organisational loyalty and retention:

> *"When seeking to establish or develop a career, a younger person might prove restless, with less concern for the job and the organisation except as a conduit for his own career".*

Similarly, the unique accumulation of experience which older workers may be in a position to offer may be viewed either in positive or negative terms. The experience of existing older employees may be valued as it relates to particularly organisational-specific knowledge and skills:

> *"Older persons have an abundance of experience that enables them to avoid the pitfalls made by younger staff".*

> *"Long-term experience can compensate for a reduction in work rate in later years, although there is usually a greater degree of loyalty and work ethic in the older person".*

> *"There is no substitute for experience: it can't be learned as an academic subject".*

However, experience earned elsewhere may not count for as much and might indeed be taken as evidence for rigidity:

> *"A number of older candidates were rejected, not necessarily because of their age, but their entrenched views and inflexibility. They clearly intended to do the job the way they had always done it and not the way that I wanted it done".*

> *"My organisation regards experience as the enemy of innovation".*

Accordingly, the employment experience which older workers possess may be valued within the organisation, but it may form a barrier when it comes to trying to get a new job.

However, even within the organisation, the accumulation of experience may not be seen in wholly positive terms. Some respondents feel, for example, that this longer term experience (rather than age per se) makes older employees more reluctant or less confident to embrace new technology and training:

> *"Some of the older employees have a tendency to consider technology a barrier and can be difficult to encourage to take on new training".*

> *"My experience to date suggests that many older people have the ability to be trained or learn new technologies but do not necessarily have the willingness".*

It must also be remembered that this willingness or ability to learn on the part of employees will, of course, be structured at least in part by the approach taken to employee training by the organisation itself.

1.5 *Qualifying Managerial Views II: 'It Depends on the Individual'*

Managers recognise that, for a variety of reasons, people of different ages might bring different characteristics and qualities to the workplace. At different points in the life-cycle, people will tend to have developed different needs, wants and abilities arising from the accumulation of experience in work, family and other roles. However, managers may also realise that the use of age should be qualified as far as realistically possible by reference to the individual. Chronological age is not necessarily predictive of attitudinal, behavioural or physical characteristics at the individual level:

> *"I have known as many irresponsible 'older' people as 'younger' and as many younger disinterested as old".*

> *"It is up to the individual and their attitude to life. You can be old at thirty".*

> *"I am strongly of the opinion that 'age' as in 'old' is not measurable in years".*

Accordingly, there may be at least as much diversity within as between age groups, particularly as:

> *"People age and mature at different rates".*

Individual changes over time may also be of a relatively minor nature and can also be mediated by individual and/or organisational interventions:

> *"People tend to keep the same characteristics as they age".*

> *"I find that most people slow down, or may be less adaptable to change, with age - but if they are good, they stay good, regardless of age!"*

> *"As an individual you can ameliorate or amplify the effects. Likewise as an employer you can influence the 'age effects' of individuals".*

As a result it can be argued on the grounds of organisational efficiency as well as individual fairness that employers should base employment decision-making as far as possible on individual, rather than group, characteristics:

> *"Age per se should not be a criterion in any issues (selection, training etc); simply the abilities of the candidate concerned, ie, technical skills, and approach to the job (motivation, energy, flexibility, etc). The important thing to do is to measure these things on an individual level".*

Or, as one respondent put it:

> *"If you are good enough, you are old enough".*

1.6 The Preferred Age Mix

Many managers are convinced of the benefits of a mixed age workforce in order to maximise the collective skills and abilities which people of different ages can bring:

> *"I have found generally that young and old have very different strengths and qualities and it is important to have this mix in a team and organisation".*

> *"All organisations need a proper spread of age groups - wisdom and experience must be balanced with energy".*

> *"I strongly believe that successful organisations need a balance of skills and experience and hence a balance of ages".*

> *"An organisation is healthier for a spread of ages, like a big family".*

Older employees could be usefully deployed in a mentoring role to develop the talents of younger staff or to lead by example:

> *"It is vital - and always has been so - to balance virgin talent with long term experience to perpetuate success".*

> *"What is needed is a mixed age/balanced workforce so that the many admirable qualities of the older employee 'rub off' on the young".*

This pursuit of a mixed workforce could be translated into patterns of recruitment:

> *"The ideal team has a mixture of backgrounds, skills and experience, so sometimes you might prefer someone younger and sometimes someone older".*

2. Attitudes to Age Barriers in Employment

Respondents were asked a number of questions relating to their own experience in order to identify the principal patterns of age use in employment. Recruitment and selection emerges as the most significant area and the patterns and possible reasons for using age here are discussed in some detail.

2.1 Location of Obstacles

Respondents were asked to state, on a seven-point Likert scale, whether individuals might experience disadvantage in their organisation due to age in relation to recruitment, training, promotion or redundancy decision-making. The results are shown in Table 3.

Base: All respondents							
	Strongly agree %			**Neither agree nor disagree %**	**Strongly disagree %**		
	1	**2**	**3**	**4**	**5**	**6**	**7**
Recruitment	18	19	18	18	8	7	12
Training	10	12	16	25	13	11	13
Promotion	13	12	16	24	14	10	12
Redundancy	20	18	16	23	7	7	11

Table 3: Age criteria by employment stage

Managers are more likely to identify age barriers relating to organisational entry and exit rather than in respect of internal development practices. Table 3 shows that 55 per cent of managers believe that older people would have less chance of being recruited to their organisation because of their age; similarly 54 per cent believe that older employees would be more likely to be made redundant, by virtue of their age. Around one in five of all respondents indicate the strongest level of agreement that these barriers exist.

Age barriers in training and promotion are reported with varying levels of conviction by 38 per cent and 41 per cent of respondents respectively. Only a minority of managers disagree that these age obstacles apply with respect to their own organisations, illustrating the pervasive nature of the use of age in employment decision-making.

The extent and strength of these barriers will clearly vary according to the nature of the job in question. With respect to recruitment, for example, managers report the lowest incidence for scientific/technical positions and for skilled manual jobs (both 31 per cent agreement levels), possibly due to a greater tendency to rely on specific criteria relating to qualifications and experience in these areas. The highest levels of agreement (41 per cent) relate to middle management positions, possibly because of greater respondent awareness here, but also possibly due to the nature of organisational age-related career timetables.

2.2 *Personal Experience I: As an Employee*

Respondents were asked whether they believed that they had experienced any unfair disadvantage in their career due to a relatively older or younger age. Table 4 provides the results relating to job applications; promotions; training access; appraisal and redundancy.

Base: All respondents	**Source of disadvantage**					
	Too old %			**Too young %**		
	Yes	**No**	**Don't know**	**Yes**	**No**	**Don't know**
Job application	44	44	12	25	62	13
Promotion	24	67	9	30	60	9
Training	14	80	6	6	86	8
Appraisal	14	78	8	10	80	10
Redundancy	15	70	16	5	77	18

Table 4: Perceptions of personal age disadvantage

The highest levels of perceived older age disadvantage relate to recruitment: more than four in ten believe that they have experienced disadvantage due to (older) age when applying for jobs. It may be that the real levels are even higher, since many long-tenured older respondents may have had only limited experience of external applications. For example, almost two thirds of those who have been with their present employer for fewer than three years report this perceived disadvantage; this continues to decline with organisational tenure, so that only a third of those employed for over ten years feel the same way.

Levels of perceived personal age disadvantage concerning training, appraisal and redundancy were relatively minor. Around a quarter of respondents, however, believe that they have experienced age barriers in promotion.

The comments of respondents support the view that age may be most significant in terms of actually getting a job:

> *"There are fewer problems once within an organisation. The problem is getting an opportunity to be considered if you are over 35".*

> *"My experience of 'age prejudice', and that of most others I suspect, is not a denial of equal opportunity once inside an organisation, it is the difficulty of getting an interview in the first instance - at the recruitment stage skills, abilities and experience appear to be secondary to age".*

This could be related to the greater scope and, indeed, need to rely on general information at the recruitment stage. Once inside an organisation there may be more objective, valid and individual-related performance information available on which to base decision-making.

The figures in Table 4 also indicate that ageism might be felt by the relatively young, as age might be taken to indicate a relative inexperience for recruitment or promotion. A quarter of all respondents believe that they have experienced age discrimination on grounds of a relatively young age when applying for a job and between a quarter and a third with respect to internal promotion.

Table 5 provides an age breakdown of responses which shows further details of reported young or old disadvantage according to respondent age. These figures show how widely age discrimination is felt by both younger and older respondents, especially in relation to recruitment and promotion.

Employment area/ reason	% agreeing			
	Under 35	35-44	45-54	55+
Job application				
too old	9	32	49	50
too young	60	33	23	16
Promotion				
too old	4	14	26	34
too young	54	40	28	19
Training				
too old	6	9	15	16
too young	15	6	6	4
Appraisal				
too old	7	10	14	19
too young	21	14	9	5
Redundancy				
too old	3	11	16	19
too young	7	8	4	4

Table 5: Perceived personal disadvantage by age and reason

The figures show, for example, that of managers under the age of 35, fully 60 per cent feel that they have been denied access to jobs because of a relatively younger age, and 54 per cent denied a promotion opportunity. Such barriers may be less commonly perceived for training, appraisal or redundancy.

Similarly, half of those in the 45 plus age groups feel that they may have been denied access to jobs because they were deemed too old and a third feel the same way over a promotion opportunity. The figures also suggest that those in the 35- 44 range could feel themselves simultaneously too young and too old for jobs, with a third of managers in this age group reporting age disadvantage on either grounds.

2.3 Personal Experience: As a Manager

Respondents were asked whether age had ever been a consideration in their decision-making concerning employee recruitment, promotion, training or redundancy/dismissal. Table 6 shows that managers may be more likely to take account of age in relation to recruitment and selection decision-making, and that a majority (55 per cent) have done so in the past. A majority of managers report that they have not used age in the other areas, although between a quarter and a third have done so.

Base: All respondents	Age Use		
Issue	**Yes %**	**No %**	**Not applicable %**
Recruitment/selection	55	41	4
Redundancy/dismissal	32	55	13
Promotion	29	66	5
Training	25	72	3

Table 6: Use of age by respondents in decision-making

These answers are not related to respondent age. Managers in larger organisations, however, may be more likely to have used age when making recruitment and redundancy/dismissal decisions.

Candidate age is therefore extensively used to inform decisions, especially in recruitment, even though the provision of training for managers in recruitment and selection is quite widespread. Nearly half of the respondents (46 per cent) report that they have received training in recruitment and selection techniques in their present organisations and more than six in ten in a prior organisation. In all, two thirds (66%) have received such training either from their present or previous employer. This could suggest that age issues are neglected in managerial training in recruitment and selection skills and techniques.

2.4 Age and Recruitment and Selection

2.4.1 Patterns in the Use of Age

Organisational patterns

Managers believe that age is more likely to be used informally rather than as a formal criterion in recruitment and selection decision-making: 53 per cent of respondents believe that age is used informally in their organisations and 32 per cent report its formal use. Both formal and informal usage is reported more widely in larger organisations, particularly where overall employment levels are decreasing. This could be because small and medium size enterprises (SMEs) may be more flexible in their recruitment patterns and methods, as procedures are reported to be more highly formalised by managers in larger organisations.

There are no significant differences between public and private sector respondents regarding the formal and informal use of age. Previous research has suggested that age barriers in recruitment might be more extensive in the private sector, both explicitly [3], and further into the selection process [1]. This is reflected in the experience of one respondent:

> *"Returning to the UK after 15 years abroad, I had to seek employment at the age of 40. I encountered a quite different attitude from potential private sector employers. I was clearly 'too old'. I benefited from the increasing of the maximum age for application to the Civil Service Direct Competition from 26 to 40, and I caught up fast with the younger people in the same year. I have had no public sector discrimination on the grounds of age, I'm happy to say".*

According to another respondent, age may be more likely to be used when third party intermediaries become involved:

> *"A lot of age discrimination is carried out by agencies when screening candidates for inward presentation".*

Overall, age barriers for organisational entry are reported more extensively by respondents in private industry [10] than the private services sector, and in organisations which are reducing employment levels, especially if through early retirement and age-related redundancy.

Analyses also indicate that age barriers may also be more pronounced where work pressures are increasing, where the existing age composition of the workforce is relatively young, and where there is perceived to be an increasing availability of suitable younger people present in the external labour market.

Accordingly, older people might find it more difficult to apply successfully for jobs which are increasing in work demands and pressures, where the existing work teams are relatively young and/or where there are plenty of younger people applying for the same position. This will particularly apply in relation to organisations which are reducing employee numbers, especially if by means of early retirement or age-related redundancy.

Personal patterns

In terms of respondents' personal characteristics, overall perceptions of age barriers are not related to respondent age. Men tend to report higher levels of age discrimination, although this can be largely accounted for by the different occupational and industrial distribution of the sexes.

Senior managers are less likely to perceive or recognise age barriers than middle or junior managers, possibly associated with their removal from the majority of routine recruitment activity. (This relationship also holds when controlling for the self-classification of managers in smaller organisations as more 'senior').

Those employed for longer with their present organisations are more likely to report age-related recruitment barriers, possibly as a result of greater organisational familiarity.

2.4.2 The Legitimacy of Using Age

Respondents were asked whether "Age can be a justifiable consideration" in recruitment and selection decision-making in their organisation. Fifty per cent of respondents agree with the statement whereas 30 per cent disagree. The pattern of responses are unrelated to most organisational and personal classification variables, including age, although respondents in larger organisations and in certain industries (particularly the armed and emergency services) tend to agree more strongly. The possible reasons for using age in recruitment and selection are explored below.

2.4.3 Accounting for Recruitment Barriers

Perceptions of organisational age discrimination are unrelated to managerial views of older workers, either in general or within the organisation, except for those relating to employment costs which are characteristics determined directly by the organisation itself.

The stereotypical views which managers hold of older workers are therefore not directly associated with organisational practice. As mediators of organisational practice, this could suggest that the reasons for any age barriers lie less with the (perceived) characteristics of older workers themselves, than with a set of different institutional processes on the demand side for labour. Although stereotypes might be relevant at the individual level, particularly in relation to certain jobs, the overall patterns of discrimination may be more likely to be formed by the nature of the organisation and the processes of organisational change. In order to test this hypothesis, respondents were provided with a number of possible 'explanations' for age barriers to the recruitment of relatively older people. Their levels of agreement or disagreement in relation to their own organisation, are detailed in Table 7 [11].

Base: All respondents							
	Strongly agree %			Neither agree nor disagree %	Strongly disagree %		
	1	2	3	4	5	6	7
Convenience of age as applicant filter	11	15	22	25	10	7	12
Customary recruitment patterns	8	11	19	35	11	6	10
Age stereotypes	11	16	19	31	7	6	9
Downsizing focus on older employees	12	12	16	33	10	7	10
Career/succession/ manpower planning	9	15	23	29	10	6	8
Age of existing work teams	9	15	23	30	9	7	8
Jobs associated with certain ages	9	15	25	25	9	8	9
Interviewer age	7	15	19	32	10	8	10
Focus on school-leavers/ recent graduates	8	11	16	28	12	12	13
Seniority pay/benefits systems	7	12	15	32	13	10	12
Availability of younger people	5	10	18	40	12	7	10
Limited recruitment activity	20	20	22	23	6	4	5
Previous salaries of older applicants	10	15	18	6	12	9	10

....continued overleaf

Pension rules/costs	8	11	15	32	11	8	14
Fixed retirement age	15	16	17	27	8	7	10
Job demands/pace of change	8	18	27	24	9	6	8
Customer expectations	2	5	12	37	15	14	15
Trade unions	2	2	5	39	8	14	31
Shortage of older applicants	3	6	12	30	18	17	15

Table 7: Explanations for age barriers in recruitment

There is a substantial level of agreement with each of the possible explanations provided, although not all will be relevant to every type of organisation. (The average level of agreement was 39 per cent).

The results suggest that the most significant reasons for age discrimination could be associated with the convenience of age as a device to filter applicants and the nature of customary patterns of recruitment.

These factors may also be related to the third most important reason, the operation of age stereotypes. Stereotypes are, therefore, important in accounting for age discrimination, alongside institutional processes such as any downsizing focus on older workers (which could make the recruitment of older people appear incongruous) and the operation of career, succession or manpower planning systems. Existing age profiles also appear relevant in potentially excluding older applicants. A majority (53 per cent) of respondents agree that job demands could serve to limit the recruitment of older people, although this is a less significant potential predictor of overall organisational discrimination. Customer expectations and the activity of trade unions appear to be less relevant. A shortage of older applicants cannot explain organisational age discrimination (hence the low position in the table) but one in five managers report that this could be a reason for any low levels of older worker recruitment in practice.

These findings are supported by the experiences and observations of managers themselves. These observations on the possible reasons for using age reflect the strength of feeling and personal experience of managers on this issue and they are discussed in some detail below.

Taken together this qualitative material provides a range of insights in support of and in addition to the statistical results discussed above.

2.4.4 Explaining age discrimination: Managerial views

Comments tend to relate to three main areas: stereotypes; age profiles and the nature of the job.

a) **Stereotypes**

Respondents suggest that age may be used as a quick and convenient indicator of a number of personal characteristics. When it is used in a negative way respondents may believe that this could also relate to a wider ageism in society as a whole.

(i) *Age as a Proxy*

Age can be used as an indicator of attitudes, experience, physical abilities or family circumstances. This latter issue, for example, might serve to benefit some men in the age range 25-45 as they may be assumed to be more hard working and ambitious for family reasons, but it may lead to further discrimination against women on the same grounds:

"Responsibility etc is more a function of wives, children, mortgages etc which tend to come with age, but are not really a direct function of age".

"I think being 'older' and with young children brings great discrimination. One is viewed as less flexible, less committed to working and less loyal to the firm because young children - as apposed to grown up children - give priorities in conflict with total dedication to the needs and demands of the employer".
(woman, 42)

Age might especially be used as a proxy device where a recruiting manager has little knowledge of the individual concerned, or limited prior experience of working with older workers in general:

"Age is not a consideration when I'm dealing with a known person or group of people. However when seeking a new contact with no recommendation, age would influence my judgement as to the suitability of the person or persons being considered".

"Until I had more direct experience of working with older people over the last 3-5 years I would have assumed older people were less flexible or willing to change. In fact I have discovered that they are more prepared, willing and understanding of the need for change and are happy to put forward positive suggestions".

It might also be the case that younger recruiters may be more likely to use age as a proxy indicator:

"The biggest impediment to the recruitment of older - and frequently well trained and highly motivated people is the age and perceptions of junior personnel practitioners who carry out - at least - the preliminary sieves of applications".

The use of age in this way might be related to the nature of the recruitment and selection process itself. As an exercise in judgement it can be as much an art as a science and this provides a wide scope for the use of subjective criteria such as age, especially where procedures may not be systematically defined. As one respondent, for example, observed:

"Fitting the appropriate people to jobs they are suited for is usually more influenced by chance than good, impartial selection and assessment methods".

(ii) *Ageism in Society*

Some managers point out that the use of age in employment is but one form of age regulation which begins with the education system and ends with retirement:

"Age related considerations stem from our social structures".

Ageism in employment may also be related to a wider negative set of cultural attitudes relating to ageing and the aged. This might be felt to have intensified with the increased accent on youth and the informalisation of social relationships which may be particularly associated with the 1960s and again reasserted in the 1980s:

"Ageism is not limited to the employment environment ... following the sixties, older people come to be regarded as no longer respectable by virtue of their seniority".

"The eighties trend to turn away from the experienced, mature workforce has been shortsighted. The'yuppie' movement was shallow".

b) **Existing Age Profiles**

Respondents acknowledge that existing age profiles may also be important in explaining the use of age in recruitment and selection. This could occur firstly in a formal sense at the organisational level in the management of internal labour markets through, for example, succession or manpower planning systems. Some respondents also assert that age bias may operate informally through a consideration of the implications of age relationships between individuals in existing work teams or between supervisors and subordinates.

(i) *Succession Planning*

Many respondents believe that the recruitment of younger people could be necessary for long-term development and for further promotions beyond the immediate job:

"I'm not discriminating on age per se, but it is important to consider age particularly during recruitment and promotion. It is essential to recruit younger staff in order to provide succession planning for the future and long-term continuity".

"There is a need to have a relatively smooth age profile for career progression, pension funding and general organisational vitality".

"Age is important if there is a requirement for long term development".

One recent effect of recession might have been to have reinforced the exclusion of older potential recruits for reasons of succession and developmental planning. This might particularly have applied to the larger organisations. These organisations may have increasingly looked to focus external recruitment on the entry level positions in order to ensure developmental continuity within this context of generally reduced recruitment activity. As one respondent remarked:

"The company has a very strong policy now to only recruit and train new graduates".

Age profiles can also, however, be a relevant consideration in smaller organisations, particularly where the existing age profile may be ageing due to reduced recruitment activity. This can similarly encourage a tendency to focus on younger entrants in order to ensure a smoother process of replacement and succession:

"A high proportion of staff will reach retirement age within the next decade - this tends to lead to recruiting relatively young staff to redress the age imbalance".

"I have 20 people directly under my control, of which just 5 are under 50. This concerns me because I need to plan ahead to replace the over 50s in the next few years (in my organisation people tend to retire early)".

However, continuing pressures to contain costs and to employ fewer people can be a constraint in attempting to respond to internal demographic changes:

"As a stable organisation we face a problem of ageing together - 75 per cent are over 40. We would like a better spread of ages, but expect to reduce numbers rather than recruit staff over the next five years".

"There has been little induction of a younger workforce. It is now top-heavy with an older staff structure... I would welcome the opportunity to train a successor if only my company would employ one!"

Some respondents are also concerned that a relatively mature age profile could also bring with it 'promotion blockages' and motivation problems with the younger staff:

"Although older employees in my organisation are extremely capable, their high proportion relative to overall numbers does lead to frustration and resentment amongst younger employees due to lack of promotion opportunities. A high turnover of younger staff exists".

Accordingly, the presence of a relatively high proportion of older employees could in certain circumstances serve as a barrier to the further recruitment of older workers for reasons of developmental and career continuity. An ageing workforce profile can present a number of potential problems for managers which may be difficult to resolve. As one respondent put it,for example:

"The mature profile is in part frustrating our younger brethren ... how do we use the 'older heads' to best effect while bringing on the 'younger bloods'?"

Finally, one of the most important institutional barriers to the recruitment of those in their late 50s and beyond may be formed by fixed retirement ages. These can serve to limit the effectiveness of investing in relatively older people, especially for those positions requiring a heavy training investment, longer term development or succession. As one respondent remarked:

"It's no use recruiting or promoting someone when they are about to retire".

In similar terms, one respondent observed that:

"Where 'potential' is required older applicants are not necessarily suitable".

(ii) *Organisational 'Age Timetables'*

The development of internal labour markets, especially in the larger organisations, serves to focus external recruitment on the entry level positions. As a result, as one manager explained:

"We only recruit at graduate and school-leaver level and promote from within".

This practice can also lead to the construction of a set of age-associated markers for subsequent job and career progression. This structure may be presented in its most well developed form, for example, in the armed services:

"I work with the RAF which of course does not recruit other than from base level so we tend to have a very junior workforce ... rank tends to go hand in hand with age, ie you have to be of a certain age before you can be considered for some promotions".

The subsequent construction of these post-entry age ladders has important implications for existing older employees as well as closing many doors to potential older recruits. One manager makes this perfectly clear:

"If people are older than their target ('still assistant manager at 50') then there is a presumption either of incompetence or lack of ambition".

Another respondent draws attention to how these age timetables can also form obstacles to younger workers in terms of organisational entry or development:

"Many persons with abilities, vision and talent who are under 30 are denied a position because they are too young - 'time-serving' is a malaise! Equally, many older employees are parked in deadend jobs because their fuel tanks are considered to be empty. They are then left to await (early) retirement and to become cynical".

The line drawn between 'too old' and 'too young' may be a particularly fine one. Some individuals report having faced problems, for example, of being both too old and too young when it comes to applying for jobs:

"At 38 years of age I have found it extremely frustrating to be considered too old for some positions and too young for others (75/25). I am now in a position of forced self- employment".

Unfortunately, it could be that one effect of the continuing flattening of organisational hierarchies might be to compress these age timetables still further. Already, as one respondent notes:

"You start off too young and rapidly become too old. If only we could all be 24-32, it seems!"

(iii) *Age 'Fit'*

Age barriers may also be formed because of a preference by managers for the recruitment of younger subordinate staff:

"Most people do not want their staff (ie those who they directly manage/supervise) to be older than they are".

"There is a natural tendency for managers to appoint staff younger than themselves".

This could be for a variety of positive or negative reasons: in order to establish mentoring relationships for development, promotion or succession; to clarify seniority relationships of power or authority; or because of concerns relating to potential rivalry or challenges from experienced subordinates. On this latter point, one respondent commented that:

"In my experience it is the mature managers who tend to discriminate against older potential recruits. This is possibly because older potential recruits are more experienced and more capable than the interviewing manager".

An alternative viewpoint was expressed by another respondent:

"The biggest obstacle is the trend to a younger aged executive and senior management who are uncomfortable with the idea of recruiting people who are older than themselves".

Questions of horizontal age 'fit' may also be considered in relation to existing work teams. These age profiles could particularly be seen as relevant if that profile is already biased to a particular age group. As one respondent explained:

"In a primarily young environment, experience has shown that an older person will drop out quickly simply because they feel uncomfortable in the situation. I take this into consideration when recruiting and if all else is equal I will probably take the younger person. This is not discrimination, simply drawing on experience".

c) **Job Requirements and Pace of Change**

The third set of barriers raised by managers relate particularly to the nature and demands of the job in question.

(i) *New Technology*

Younger people may be advantaged if they are in possession of the most up to date qualifications and relevant skills. This might particularly apply in relation to new and/or rapidly expanding technological fields, where the recency of full-time education for the young can give them a head-start:

"We specialise in design and R&D in all areas of technology (35 per cent of us have PhD's) - We recruit young, active people with new ideas and expect them to continue their development with us".

"Young graduates have a good knowledge of the use of new advanced software, which is a great advantage".

The experience and qualifications which older people can offer may appear, in contrast, out of date:

"Problems are not solely related to age, but the training and qualifications held by older employees which are inadequate today".

"Change means that experience is becoming a less valued commodity".

(ii) *Work Intensification*

Organisational rationalisation and restructuring, in a context of increasing competition and job insecurity, now commonly means that the demands of work are increasing. Older workers may be perceived to be less able and/or willing to cope with these increased workloads:

"Many employers are looking more and more to younger employees as layers of management are cut away leaving heavier workloads and longer hours to those left. It is believed that the younger managers will be more prepared to take this on lower pay".

"Managers are informally expected to work 70 hours to be making any sort of contribution. This does have a 'burn out' effect in respect of retention of middle management".

It might be the case that as individual needs and wants from work change, older workers might be less prepared to accept such pressures. As one respondent commented, for example:

"At 42 I had a big mortgage and two sons at University. I worked hard for a lot of money. At 57 the house and children are paid for and 'quality of life' is now very important".

(iii) *Physical Jobs*

In some physical occupations, younger workers may be required of necessity, although it may still be the case that a broader age range is considered in other parts of the organisation:

"We supply a fitting service to domestic public sector housing managers. The vast majority of our workforce therefore have to be physically very fit and strong to carry our products. This leads to the average age being under thirty. Our admin offices do employ across a broad age range".

"Installation work is not considered suitable for the more mature. However with regard to supervision etc we believe that there is considerable benefit in employing the more mature".

"Our main age-related problem is the back! - In manual departments older people are a problem. In other areas experience has great value".

Similar reservations may apply to sustained fast-paced work such as manufacturing processing. As one manager explained:

"We have had older people from employment agencies and the majority of them find it difficult to keep pace with the younger workers".

(iv) *Few Job Applications*

Such job characteristics as the physical or technological nature of the work could mean that older people are less attracted or in a position to apply. In these circumstances the low representation of older workers may not be designed nor necessarily desired by management:

"In my experience it is often difficult to get older people to apply for positions. This may be related to the nature of the work (lorry driving for example)".

"We only have a limited number of older people who apply to work in the factory although we believe a mixture of ages is vital".

"Age is not a concern in the software industry. If we were presented with a 65 year old that had computer programming experience then we would hire him. The main problem seems to be one of skills and the attitude to learn this new technology".

d) **Employment Costs**

The cost of employing older workers may be seen as a direct consideration in recruitment due for example to age related seniority pay and benefit structures, or a more indirect consideration in relation for example to previous salaries. Age and experience linked payment systems appear to be a potential obstacle particularly in the education sector:

"Older teachers command a higher salary and, with local management of schools, governors take cost as a factor before qualifications".

"In education generally, and in my Further Education College, because of the nature of the contract of employment for lecturing staff, older people are more expensive to employ. Also, because they can carry forward their service in any educational establishment, they are more expensive when redundancy is necessary".

More indirectly, it could be the case that younger workers at all levels may be more prepared (or possibly better able) to accept lower salaries in return, for example, for the opportunity to accumulate training or experience. Organisations may be turning to younger people as part of cost-cutting strategy as a result:

"I have witnessed older, experienced accountants being got rid of and replaced by inexperienced younger accountants purely on a financial basis".

"Younger employees are taken on because they are cheap".

"The experience and stability that the more mature employees can offer is discarded because the younger are cheaper".

Some older workers may, however, be in a position to compete on pay. As one respondent points out for his organisation:

"These young are being sought for cheapness; also the older 'second careerists' also for cheapness, because they have paid off houses, acquired savings and have pension means etc".

Other individuals might have to revise their pay expectations, whatever their age:

"After being made redundant, age 36, due to a cost-saving rationalisation, I took six months to find another job. Seventy applications returned a lot of rejections - some didn't bother to reply, some stipulated 'too old'. I accepted a reduced salary in order to start, and received the first job offers: three in one week!. Being made to feel you are on the scrapheap at 35 is ridiculous but a fact of life right now".

From the organisational point of view, however, a concentration solely on direct and immediate costs may be counter-productive in the longer term. As one respondent points out:

"In general older employees cost more - this is a barrier, but not an insurmountable one. It is my experience that this extra cost is more than compensated for by increasing flexibility and effort".

e) **Customer Expectations**

Within the service sector and particularly in some areas of retailing which may be targeted at young markets it may be seen as important to recruit younger people in order to match staffing to the customer profile. One respondent points out, for example, that:

"The company's 'target customer' is under forty and it is taken as read that customers want to be served by someone near their own age, although I know of no research having been carried out to either support or refute this theory. Experience tends to suggest that customers are not greatly interested in the age or gender of the person serving them, however this is difficult to prove to senior management who are, in any case, well under forty!"

Nevertheless, such a human resourcing strategy could be argued for on business grounds and has been conversely applied to the older employee, most notably by B&Q in the DIY sector [12].

f) **Labour Market Competition**

Reinforcing all the above factors may be the fact of increasing competition in the labour market and the continued and increasing availability of suitable younger workers for jobs of all types. As one respondent observed:

"There are so many well qualified people around now at lower ages with supposedly more energy".

2.4.5 Future Recruitment of Older Workers

Respondents were asked to indicate their expectations of older worker recruitment by their organisations for the medium term. The results are shown in Table 8.

Base: All Respondents			
	Increase (%)	**About the same (%)**	**Decrease (%)**
Recruitment of older people	17	47	36
Proportion of older employees	23	47	30
Average workforce age	35	38	27

Table 8: Medium term expectations of older worker employment

Less than one in five managers (17 per cent) expect their organisation to increase the recruitment of older individuals over the coming few years. This perception is not related to respondent age, nor to any personal views of the relative merits of older workers. However, further analysis shows that managers in smaller organisations appear to be much more confident concerning the future recruitment of older workers.

This is primarily because such managers tend to be more confident about increasing the levels of employment overall. In addition, they may also feel well placed to benefit from the displacement of skilled older workers and managers from other larger organisations. In the words of one respondent:

> *"There is a great reservoir of business skills and experience at both middle and senior management levels not now employed due to 'delayering' etc, especially from bigger companies. This skill can be harnessed to support and mentor SMEs so that we can make significant gains in performance".*

Another factor which could determine the future levels of older worker recruitment is the age composition of the internal and external labour markets. Analyses indicate, for example, that recruitment may be more likely where the existing organisational profile is already mixed or mature rather than young. Managers in these organisations may have fewer reservations concerning the work abilities of older people due to their greater familiarity with older people in the workforce (although the potential barrier formed by a particularly ageing profile discussed above should also be noted). These managers could also have fewer doubts concerning the ability of older people to fit into the existing work teams. Secondly, anticipated recruitment increases where managers expect the availability of suitable younger labour to be decreasing, suggesting that in some cases older workers may be viewed as a reserve or substitute labour pool.

Table 8 also shows that although less than one in five managers expect the recruitment of older people to increase, over a third believe that the average age of the workforce will increase. This reflects the generally reduced level of external recruitment activity and a possible stabilisation of employment levels in the short to medium term. However, over a quarter of respondents anticipate the average workforce age to decrease and three in ten believe that the proportion of older employees will decrease. This may be a measure of the continued use of early retirement and other age related redundancy schemes where there is a need to reduce the size of the workforce.

It is possible that the increasing fragmentation of traditional career structures could open up opportunities for skilled older workers through self-employment and temporary contract working. Age can be less of a relevant consideration for managers when employing on a non-permanent basis. As one respondent put it:

> *"I am increasing my reliance on agency workers. Age, sex etc is not considered here".*

The expansion of 'second career' and 'post-career' employment opportunities, including for example in the voluntary sector, education or SMEs might involve less regular and often less well paid employment. This may be balanced by an expansion of family or leisure time and possibly greater independence concerning work. Whether this is considered advantageous overall obviously depends on the circumstances, needs and wants of the individual. It is possible that the polarisation between those empowered and those marginalised by increased employment flexibility will itself increase. Since this position will be determined in large part by the relevance and marketability of individual skills it is imperative that individuals, organisations and other players such as the TECs act to ensure the continual development of the skills of workers of all ages.

2.5 Age and Training and Promotion

Respondents were asked for details about the quantity and perceived quality of training provided for them by the organisations. The average training received by managers in the previous twelve months is seven days. Over a quarter (27 per cent) state that they received no job related training, and a further quarter (24 per cent) received between one and four days. Training tends to be directed towards younger managers: 18 per cent of those under age 35 for example received no training at all, compared to 22 per cent of those aged 35-44; 32 per cent of those aged 45- 54 and 40 per cent of those aged 55 or over.

This will, of course, be related to the greater developmental needs of younger, more junior, managers. However when controlling statistically for the effects of occupational level, there remains a significant negative partial correlation between age and the amount of training received. This implies that older managers may receive less training than younger managers even when we take account of the greater job-related training needs of the latter group.

This could indicate that older workers receive less training because of their age, storing up problems for both the individual and the organisation for the future. One relatively young (age 33) respondent points out that directing training opportunities away from older workers can be counter-productive. The greater employment stability of older workers can mean, for example, a greater payback period on the initial training investment, the depreciation rate of which is in any case increasing due to the pace of technological and other change in the workplace:

> *"I think that there is much short-sightedness regarding 'older' workers. Companies cannot see much further that five years, so what is the problem about employing older workers? After all they can be more reliable and as for being set in their ways, that just requires good people management".*

The average rating of training received by managers is six marks out of a possible ten. The evaluation of training is positively related to the amount received, suggesting that quality and quantity in training provision is related. When controlling for the amount of training received by respondents, so that we can take account in the analysis of the greater provision of training for younger managers, we discover that overall the perception of training quality is unrelated to age. Accordingly, there is no evidence to suggest that the quality of training provided is different for employees of different ages.

The processes of organisation restructuring and change which have served in many cases to reduce entry opportunities for older workers may also lead to diminishing opportunities in developmental terms.

Compulsory retirement ages have long placed a limit on the potential contribution of older employees, but this age ceiling on training may effectively be lowering as a result of early retirement programmes. As one respondent put it:

> *"Older people increasingly tend to retire early and in certain cases this is good for them and good for the organisation. But it means that in some cases investing in an employee over, say, fifty may give a very poor return".*

The process of delayering, together with reductions in the overall size of the workforce, has also served to withdraw the traditional career ladder from many employees. This could mean that effective age limits on promotions may be occurring at earlier ages:

> *"Promotion has now stopped for anyone over 35. The organisational structure has gone from 11 to 6 and career patterns are dramatically reduced".*

> *"Promotion has now become virtually non-existent. People who leave are generally not replaced and their workloads are shared out".*

Added to the effects of these change processes are increasing cost concerns and a shortening of the planning horizon which can encourage a tendency to buy-in ready made skills rather than to develop them internally over the longer term:

> *"Retraining is viewed as expensive and new expertise tends to be bought in, especially at middle management level".*

Accordingly, training and promotion opportunities for many older workers and others may be decreasing, not necessarily as a result of negative attitudes concerning the abilities of older employees, but due to the effects of organisational cost-cutting, rationalisation and restructuring.

This raises the danger of the 'plateaued' manager by which the prophecy of older employee demotivation and stagnation is self-fulfilled through an increasing denial of internal development opportunities with age.

This requires organisational recognition and active intervention in order to prevent a vicious circle from developing, for, as one respondent put it:

> *"The 'left on the shelf' scenario must be discouraged to enhance participation, interest and to maintain the will to continue to produce in senior age staff and senior age middle management in particular".*

The development of flexible career structures for managerial and professional staff could help to limit this problem. This could take the form of cross-functional project working and horizontal patterns of career development, allied to the continual training of all existing employees:

> *"As employment opportunities at middle and senior management levels will at best remain static, more emphasis should be placed on moving horizontally between job functions. In this environment, would impart enormous benefits in terms of departmental interworking".*

One practical step which individuals of all ages could adopt would be to maintain up to date and accurate records of developmental achievements. One respondent recommends that this should be given at least a formal endorsement by organisations:

> *"A 'Continuous Professional Development' register (logbook etc) should be mandatory for all professionals and managers".*

2.6 *Age, Redundancy and Early Retirement*

Declining employment levels are most commonly reported by respondents in the larger organisations. The biggest proportionate reductions appear to have been experienced by the utilities and communications industries, and in the emergency/armed services. Expectations of future employment growth are most widely reported by contrast in the SME sector.

Table 9 indicates the extent and form of downsizing efforts by type of organisation.

	All %	Public sector %	Plc %	Private company %	Owner managed/ partnership %
Downsizing	67	84	83	61	33
Downsizing which is focused on older workers	58	40	31	22	3
Early retirement	54	86	70	37	15
Voluntary redundancy	52	80	72	37	16
Compulsory redundancy	46	49	61	45	23

Table 9: Extent and form of downsizing within the last 5 years

The impact of increased competition and recession is shown by the fact that over two thirds of managers in the sample report efforts to reduce the size of the workforce in the last five years. This has been most pronounced in the larger organisations where more than eight in ten respondents report efforts to reduce the size of the workforce. Most of these organisations are also likely to focus on older workers in order to manage the downsizing programme of workforce reduction, especially through the use of early retirement and voluntary redundancy. This is enabled in the larger organisations by the wider coverage of occupational pension schemes in these organisations. It might also be related to the higher incidence of trade unionisation which could make these schemes more attractive in industrial relations terms.

Further analyses indicate that respondents in larger organisations also appear to anticipate greater changes in the nature and organisation of work. They are more likely to expect, for example, continued work intensification and the introduction of more flexible working practices in the form of task flexibility, multi-skilling and part-time and temporary contracting. This quest for further flexibility is likely to be maintained in a context of increasing job insecurity and additional work pressures. In these circumstances early retirement might appear additionally attractive to older employees as well as delivering a number of possible advantages to the organisations concerned.

2.6.1 Focusing on Older Employees: Merits and Disadvantages

Respondents were asked whether their organisation "should focus on older employees as a means of reducing headcount". Almost eight in ten (79 per cent) disagree with such a policy (14 per cent agree and 6 per cent don't know). There are no age, sex, occupational or organisational patterns to this response except that those in favour are more likely to be located in organisations which have initiated such a policy. They also tend to have a poorer overall new of the work capabilities and effectiveness of older employees in their organisation.

a) **Advantages**

Some of the main organisational advantages of an age-related scheme for reducing workforce numbers were delivered to the sample and the responses are shown in Table 10. Such a scheme might be favoured, for example, because it can meet employee aspirations for early retirement. It could also bring other benefits by opening promotion channels, reducing the need for compulsory redundancies and by an ability to be financed out of pension funds. These programmes can also be practical to operate and can result in significant salary savings by concentrating on the most expensive (but not necessarily the least productive) employees. As might be expected, all of these reasons are seen as more appropriate by respondents in the larger organisations. There is no relationship to any respondent personal characteristics, including individual age.

Base: All respondents			
	Agree %	Neither agree nor disagree %	Disagree %
Meet aspirations for early retirement	64	22	14
Open up promotion channels	48	23	29
Can finance through pension funds	42	38	20
Concentrate on most expensive employees	42	25	33
Practical to operate	41	34	25
Reduce the need for compulsory redundancies	41	33	26
Reduce wider workforce opposition	29	38	34
Concentrate on less productive employees	26	25	50

Table 10: Advantages of age-related downsizing

Additional comments from respondents suggest that, in certain circumstances, such programmes can serve to benefit early retirees and the remaining employees in addition to the organisation itself. Firstly, such programmes can benefit older workers themselves by meeting a desire for early retirement, especially on favourable terms:

> *"In my experience many older workers are very content (and often ask) to be released in their early fifties to be able to do the things they have always wanted to do".*

> *"Older workers in our organisation more often want early retirement as they receive a better package".*

However it is recognised that there could be negative reasons for wanting release in addition to those relating to the financial package and improved leisure opportunities:

> *"The organisation has a predominantly older workforce who through pressures of work are waiting for some kind of scheme which will allow them to retire early (50+). Jobs are becoming generally harder".*

> *"People are more influenced by the increased pressure and amount of change".*

The voluntary nature of participation in such schemes might also be compromised as older employees realise that any favourable terms could be reduced or withdrawn at a later date. Many are also actively encouraged or induced to take up the offer. In one organisation, for example:

> *"All employees nearing 50 are approached with an early retirement offer".*

Secondly, and as discussed above, these schemes can benefit the organisation by facilitating a less disruptive means of transition. In the experience of one respondent:

> *"Voluntary redundancy and early retirement being available to the over-fifties has enabled re-organisation(s) to be managed without causing too much trauma".*

Thirdly, such programmes can also benefit the majority remaining employees by reducing the need for compulsory redundancy and so enabling them to keep their jobs. As such these initiatives may be seen as the least unfair mechanism for managing downsizing overall:

> *"Early retirement can be a 'humane' way of downsizing an organisation in that younger workers keep their jobs and the 'victims' get their pension paid sooner than expected".*

The same respondent points out, however, that:

> *"This may not be in the best long-term interest of the organisation if valuable experience is lost".*

b) **Disadvantages**

Comments from respondents also indicate that a number of organisational costs can be incurred in the use of early retirement to manage a process of workforce reduction, particularly in the medium to longer term. The largest of these potential problems relates to the loss of skilled and experienced personnel:

"In recent years we are aware that we are deskilling our organisation by losing staff through voluntary redundancy, but it's seen as the 'painless' way out".

"There is a serious risk of the organisation losing staff with extensive knowledge over a very short period".

"We have bitterly regretted losing many of the folk who have gone in the last five years and have even refused some redundancy applications".

The loss of experienced older employees could also have a number of negative implications for the remaining employees. The focus of these voluntary redundancy and early retirement initiatives on reducing employee numbers and making salary savings at the higher levels could mean that applications are not closely managed on a job or individual basis. As one respondent points out, this could result in a poorer quality of work directly through the loss of skilled and experienced personnel, and indirectly by increasing the pressures on those left behind:

"Although voluntary redundancy is available to all, the financial has allowed older employees, many of whom were key members of staff, to leave. There is now a severe dearth of relevant skills and experience in certain functional divisions and this is causing major difficulties, more or less forcing the remaining workforce to work long hours under continual pressure in a belated effort to cope".

Another set of problems may occur in time since when combined with limited recruitment activity this encouragement of older workers to leave could serve to concentrate the age profile in the middle ranges. This could lead to longer term problems in relation to promotion, employee motivation, succession and the management of retirement:

"Voluntary redundancy has, with very low levels of recruitment, changed the age profile of the company. In a few years, if there is only limited recruitment at intake, the company will become increasingly 'middle aged'".

"We are storing up a very flat age profile which will cause problems in years to come".

Referring back to Table 8, over a third of respondents (35 per cent) anticipate the average age of the workforce to increase in the coming few years (38 per cent expect stability), possibly as this age cohort begins to advance through the organisation.

A final negative consideration may be that the extensive availability of early exit can stimulate an expectation of early retirement, with possibly unhealthy implications for employee motivation. As observed by one respondent:

"As local government contracts we have discovered the T.G.I.F. Syndrome (Thank God I'm Fifty!), since at fifty or more usually fifty five, early retirement can be requested".

In conclusion, therefore, early exit programmes may or may not benefit some or all of the three interested parties (the employer, older workers and other employees) depending on the extent, form and management of the scheme. It may be, however, that the continual availability of a widespread programme will involve a number of financial and other costs to be borne by the organisation both over the short and longer term.

3. Attitudes to Age, Legislation and Equality of Opportunity

3.1 Legislation

Managerial attitudes to legislative intervention were explored at two levels. Firstly, views on legislation to restrict the use of age limits in job advertisements were examined. Secondly, attitudes to more comprehensive employment protection legislation in a form similar to that relating to race and sex discrimination were also explored. These results are shown in Table 11.

Base: All respondents	Yes %	No %	Don't know %
1. Job advertisements	69	28	3
2. Comprehensive	85	27	8

Table 11: Attitudes to legislation

Around two-thirds of respondents are in favour of either form of legislation. Nearly six in ten managers (57 per cent) are in favour of both forms of intervention, whereas only one in five (20 per cent) are opposed to both. These surprisingly high figures could be related to increased insecurity in employment and higher levels of managerial job mobility. Managers may feel that action to remove age obstacles may be personally beneficial by reducing frictions in the labour market. Accordingly these figures are fairly consistent across age groups (Table 12) and there are no statistically significant differences in overall response according to age.

Base: All respondents	Respondent Age			
	< 35 %	35-44 %	45-54 %	55 + %
1. Job advertisements	62	68	72	67
2. Comprehensive	63	63	66	63

Table 12: Attitudes to legislation by age

Managers may also be aware of the relatively early use of age limits in employment: in 1991 for example the mean upper age limit stated in job advertisements for white-collar and junior/middle management positions carried in the national press was 30 and 33 respectively [3] and 37 for all the sample as a whole (n = 874). Further research conducted in 1993 (N = 534) found the mean upper age bar to be 25 years old, and recent research conducted in 1995 confirms that most age limits are located in the 20s and 30s [13].

A majority of managers in organisations of all sizes favour legislation, including the most comprehensive alternative. Within the private sector, however, agreement is higher for respondents in the larger organisations and for those in the very smallest category (most of whom may be self-employed or in owner-managed firms or partnerships). Managers in other smaller and medium sized organisations may be more cautious as they could feel that legislation would have more of an impact on their routine employment practices than those in the very smallest or largest firms.

3.1.1 The Case for Legislation

Respondents were keen to explain their support or opposition to legislation. Managers may in the first instance already be aware of existing regulations relating to the direct and indirect use of age:

> *"HGV and PSV licences apply at a minimum age, with strict medical criteria after middle age".*

> *"Organisation policy is to not allow recruitment advertisements to mention age as this could cause sex discrimination".*

The case for further legislation to restrict the use of age may be argued for individual and/or organisational reasons, on the basis of fairness and efficiency:

> *"I feel strongly that it is morally and commercially just as indefensible as discrimination on the grounds of sex, race and/or disability".*
>
> *"Age discrimination results from an obsession with 'bright young people' and is one of the UKs major social evils, as well as an incredible waste of potentially highly productive and motivated resources".*
>
> *"I am strongly in favour of legislation against age prejudice - my older employees are my best!"*

However, many of those in favour recognise that legislation alone can be no solution to age discrimination since, as one respondent summed it up as "it is a question of attitude". Respondents are aware that although legislation may be a useful device to raise awareness or to challenge organisational practice, in reality the effects may not be immediately significant. As one respondent put it:

> *"Legislation will have little meaning because companies will still operate with upper and lower age limits but on an informal basis".*

Age legislation may also be recognised to be a more complex and potentially problematic area for legislative intervention. Age is unique in that, unlike for example race and sex, it is relative and continually changing. People move through different stages of advantage and disadvantage and this form of discrimination might therefore be less clearly recognised. Age identity may also be weak and ageing is generally perceived in negative terms, even by older people themselves. Age might also be acknowledged to be legitimate in employment for planning purposes. In addition, as age can be broadly related to experience, physical ability and family circumstances, employers may feel justified in assuming different outlooks, skills and abilities at different points in the adult life cycle. All these factors could make legislation difficult to frame and even more difficult to implement:

> *"There is a problem of age discrimination but there are also legislative problems that do not exist with race and sex, eg. what is old?; many older employees want the early retirement provisions; many older workers accept age in the working environment; older people work differently".*

In any case, as one respondent asserted:

> *"It would be difficult to prove ageism affected the decision".*

3.1.2 The Case Against

The above reservations might lead managers to oppose legislation, particularly as age may be viewed as a relevant consideration in many decisions:

> *"Some jobs suit older people, some younger people. To remove this flexibility would be an expensive and ill-considered political move".*

> *"Managers have enough problems with existing discrimination laws and, unlike racism, age can be a legitimate factor in choosing who to appoint and who to disappoint".*

Managers from smaller organisations in particular may oppose such regulations per se as another form of bureaucratic interference:

> *"Industry needs less regulations not more".*

> *"The less legislation - the better".*

Or as one respondent expressed it in more direct and forthright terms:

> *"It's my money and I'll spend it on who I like".*

Some respondents also believe that legislation could be counter productive if it leads, for example, to mere 'window dressing':

> *"I believe age ranges are sometimes necessary in recruitment. In order to ensure specific applications and to avoid timewasting all round, the age range is included in the job advert. I see this as open, honest and effective management - not age*

discrimination. I would be most concerned if I was not permitted this flexibility because of legislation".

"I am fifty and am seeking a new job on impending retirement. I find it useful to know from advertisements the age group sought, otherwise I can waste a lot of time making useless applications for jobs".

Other respondents may state opposition in the wider sense that they are "against any campaign to extend the working life of older people" on social grounds given the context of high levels of unemployment:

"The number of jobs is and will remain finite and diminishing. The only way to provide employment opportunities for the young is to lower not raise the average age at which employees retire, otherwise the social costs (including crime and disorder) will be great".

"Earlier retirement should be across the board in order to cope with the lack of opportunities for graduates and school-leavers".

"Clearly, young people with family obligations (25-45) should have priority".

Finally, some respondents point out that legislation may be unnecessary as well as ineffective or even counter productive. It may be argued, for example, that demographic changes and the successful performance of older workers within organisations will serve as alternative pressures to employ older people:

"Many organisations are consciously recruiting older people. As the birth rate drops the situation will take care of itself, ie organisations will have to look to older people".

"Demographic changes are making it imperative for organisations to recruit and train older people, although they are using age to streamline senselessly".

"The younger population is shrinking, in both numbers and quality. The skills gap is becoming serious. Market forces will override age and sex. I believe that the millennium could become the age of the 'Greys'".

Accordingly, it may well be that organisations will therefore begin to address age as an equality issue on their own terms, independently of any external legislative pressures.

3.2 Age and Equal Opportunity

Respondents were asked a number of questions relating to actual policy and practice concerning equality of opportunity and age issues in their organisations. They were also asked for their personal views of such initiatives and activity.

3.2.1 Policy and Practice

Equal Opportunity policies are widely reported by respondents, alongside training support for managers.

Written Equal Opportunity (EO) policies are reported in most organisations, although they are more likely to be in place in the public sector and, for private sector employers, to be more likely in the larger firms (see Table 13).

	Sector		
	All	**Public**	**Private**
EO policy	63 %	91 %	53 %
No. employees			
<7	14	-	14
7-24	36	50	32
25-99	46	88	39
100-499	65	89	56
500-999	74	86	68
1000-4999	77	92	68
over 5000	90	94	87

Table 15: Written EO policy, by sector and size

Age is included in 34 per cent of these written policies and again is more likely in the public (40 per cent) than private sector (30 per cent). Organisational size does not appear to be relevant to the inclusion of age in EO.

EO training is routinely provided for managers in almost half the organisations and again is more prevalent in the public (60 per cent) than the private (43 per cent) sector. Training is more likely to be provided if the organisation actually has a written EO policy (57 per cent) than if it does not have such a document (36 per cent). There is no clear relationship between organisational size and the provision of training in EO.

Training received in EO (from their present organisation) is reported by 31 per cent of respondents. This is more likely in public sector and larger organisations. Women are more likely to have received EO training than men (49 per cent and 29 per cent respectively). This could be related in part to the occupational distribution of female respondents. Only one in five (21 per cent) of managers working in a production or engineering function have received EO training, for example, whereas 60 per cent of personnel managers have done so. Women make up 1 per cent of the former group but 17 per cent of the latter.

In all, 44 per cent of respondents have received some form of EO training, either in their present or previous organisations. Analyses indicate that this is not related to managerial level nor to respondent age.

3.2.2 Views of EO Activity

Managers have a very positive view of EO activity on both business and ethical grounds (see Table 14). Respondents in the public sector and female respondents in particular may tend to hold an even more approving view.

Base: All respondents							
Equal opportunity is:	**Strongly agree %**			**Neither agree nor disagree %**	**Strongly disagree %**		
	1	**2**	**3**	**4**	**5**	**6**	**7**
Relevant to all employees	41	23	20	11	3	1	1
An important moral issue	36	26	18	15	3	1	1
An important business issue	29	22	22	17	6	3	2
Important for minority groups	31	21	16	22	4	3	4
A mainstream managerial activity	19	21	22	19	9	6	4

Table 14: Views of equal opportunity activities

Managers strongly believe that equal opportunity activity is both an important moral issue (90 per cent agree and 36 per cent agree in the very strongest terms) and an important business issue (73 per cent and 29 per cent respectively). Only one in five disagree that it is a mainstream managerial activity.

Respondents were also asked whether employers should treat age as an equality issue. A large majority (85 per cent) agree that they should. This opinion is not related to respondent age, nor any other personal or organisational characteristics except for respondent sex, as women are slightly more likely to agree (91 per cent as against the male 85 per cent).

Most of these managers believe, furthermore, that age should be of equal importance to the more conventional areas for EO activity (see Table 15).

Base: Respondents in favour of age as an EO issue			
	Age is....		
Comparative issues	**More important %**	**Equally important %**	**Less important %**
Race	18	71	12
Sex	15	76	9
Disability	13	72	15

Table 15: Importance of age compared with other equal opportunity issues

This shows that a large majority of managers support action by their own organisations to formally address the issues of age discrimination regardless of any outside legislative measures to which, in any case, they also lend their support.

Conclusions

The results show how strongly managers are aware of the relevance of age in employment. Age may be taken to indicate a range of important characteristics and it can be used in all forms of decision-making concerning organisational entry, subsequent development and exit. Age discrimination is almost as likely to be experienced by younger as by older workers.

Managers are divided when it comes to lending their approval to such practices. Many argue that it can be unfair and inefficient to focus on age whereas others believe that age can, in reality, be indicative of individual personality, experience and motivation and so can be legitimately used to manage, for example, succession and development in the organisation.

Most managers are in favour, however, of legislation to counter age discrimination. This could be related to the processes of organisational change and the fragmentation of traditional career structures. Age barriers might, for example, be experienced at earlier ages as a result of organisational delayering.

Organisational downsizing and outsourcing means that an increasing number of managers of all ages are actually or potentially exposed to those age barriers in the labour market. Accordingly, as employees, managers might oppose the use of age criteria in employment even if, as managers, they recognise certain advantages to employers in doing so.

The future is as yet unclear. Emerging patterns of flexible employment could serve to make references to age in employment decision-making irrelevant. The transitional period could, however, involve a growing polarisation between advantaged and marginalised groups in the labour market. Some groups of skilled older workers may, for example, be in a position to benefit from early retirement and be able to renegotiate a more worthwhile balance between their working and non-work lives through short-term or part-time work on a consultancy type basis. Others might find themselves effectively excluded from the labour market if their skills and experience are not longer seen as up to date.

The results highlight a variety of possible reasons for the wide-spread use of age in employment decision-making. This might vary according to different organisational patterns (eg size, sector and industry), job conditions (eg skills requirements) and individual characteristics (eg sex and age). Age discrimination in employment is, therefore, complex and difficult to explain in general terms [14].

The evidence provided in this report shows, however, the level of managerial interest and depth of feeling and concern on this issue across a range of organisations and by managers of all ages and types.

Recommendations

The following practical recommendations are detailed for both organisations and individuals.

Organisations

Recruitment and Selection

Ensure that systems are in place in order to achieve individual-centred decision-making. Test the existing processes for objectivity, from the initial job description and person specification, through to the content of the application form and advertisement and conduct of the interview itself. Examine whether a form of selection testing may be appropriate. If age is to be used, examine, justify and clearly state the rationale. Ensure that interviewing managers are trained in recruitment and selection techniques, and evaluate the regularity, content and effectiveness of this training.

Appraisal

Apply a developmentally-led competency based approach in order to ensure that all employees continuously maintain their skills and have access to training, in addition to monitoring their performance.

Mid-career counselling can be used to identify the developmental needs and preferences of employees at this important stage. A joint skills plan can be developed in order to retain and maximise their contribution to the organisation.

Development

Develop flexible forms of career development, including horizontal mobility and cross-functional project working, in order to maintain the motivation of employees.

Examine the scope for older managers and workers to formally or informally act as mentors to less experienced employees.

Employment Patterns

Pension trustees should examine, with employers, the terms of the pension funds in order to test the possibility of a flexible transition to retirement.

Examine the potential for developing a flexible 'skill bank' of retired and early retired workers. Such former employees have valuable experience of the organisation and can be used on a consultancy basis or to manage peak periods of demand.

Organisational Planning

Regularly examine age profiles across the organisation and by the various staffing grades and departments. Incorporate this database into organisational planning, for example in the assessment of future benefits, liabilities and staffing needs.

Absence, turnover and performance could also be analysed by age group in order to inform the human resource planning process.

Early Retirement

Develop a cost/benefit analysis relevant to the alternative forms of managing a downsizing process. Ensure close managerial control over the terms for early retirement, particularly concerning access, and ensure that these are clearly communicated and understood.

Equal Opportunity

Clearly state organisational antipathy towards any form of discrimination, including on grounds of age. Ensure that this is widely communicated and that managers are trained in equal opportunity issues. Ensure the translation of the commitment into day to day practice by referring to it, for example, as a possible disciplinary matter. Incorporate age into equal opportunity policies in the same manner as for sex, race and disbility.

Individuals

CPD

Individuals must continually develop their skills, taking on responsibility for their own development, which may involve personal investment. Continuing Professional Development, which allows managers to develop their own competencies and supports their career development, should be embraced by all managers.

Employability

This should be enhanced by refocusing a skill base from traditional technical skills towards the development of a range of transferable skills. These include computer literacy, interpersonal skills, communication techniques, foreign languages, team working, financial management and strategic analysis.

Appendix 1 - The Questionnaire

MANAGEMENT HOUSE
COTTINGHAM ROAD
CORBY
NORTHANTS
NN17 1TT
TELEPHONE: 0536 204222
FACSIMILE: 0536 201651

August 1995

Dear Member

AGE, CAREERS AND THE MANAGER

The UK shares, with countries worldwide, demographic trends that are producing an ageing population and workforce. At the same time, career and organisational structures are changing with an increasing emphasis on mobility and flexibility.

The significance of age in the context of careers and employment is the subject of a major research project that the Institute is conducting with Manchester Metropolitan University and I am writing to ask for your help in completing this questionnaire.

Issues will include:

- the abilities and characteristics of workers of different ages
- age and equal opportunities
- potential age barriers in employment
- personal experiences of ageism

It is important that the research is based on the views and experiences of managers of different ages, backgrounds and organisations. I do hope that you will find the time to complete the questionnaire. The information that you give will be treated in strictest confidence and all replies are anonymous.

Please return the completed questionnaire in the enclosed reply-paid envelope by **29th September 1995**. If you mislay the envelope, the return address is:

Jim Arrowsmith
Department of Management
Manchester Metropolitan University
Aytoun Building, Aytoun Street
Manchester M1 3GH

Thank you in advance for your help. The results of the research will form the basis of a report to be published in early 1996.

Yours sincerely

Roger Young
DIRECTOR GENERAL

AGE, CAREERS AND THE MANAGER

BACKGROUND: YOUR ORGANISATION

---

1. Is your organisation:

[Please tick ONE box only]

Public sector	☐	1
Public limited company	☐	2
Private limited company	☐	3
Voluntary sector	☐	4
Owner managed/partnership	☐	5
Other *[Please specify]*..	☐	6

---

2. What is the main area of activity of your organisation?

[Please tick ONE box only]

Manufacturing/processing	☐	1
Engineering	☐	2
Distribution/transport	☐	3
Retail/wholesale	☐	4
Hotel/catering/leisure	☐	5
Emergency/armed services	☐	6
Health services	☐	7
Professional/consultancy/business services	☐	8
Public administration/local government	☐	9
Construction	☐	10
Energy/water supply	☐	11
Communications	☐	12
Banking/insurance/finance	☐	13
Other services	☐	14
Education/training	☐	15
Other *[Please specify]*..	☐	16

1

3. How many employees does your organisation have in the UK?

[Please tick ONE box only]

1 - 6	☐	1
7 - 24	☐	2
25 - 99	☐	3
100 - 499	☐	4
500 - 999	☐	5
1,000 - 4,999	☐	6
Over 5,000	☐	7

4. Does your organisation have a separate Personnel/HR section?

Yes		☐	1
No	Go to Q6	☐	2

5. If YES to Q4, would you say that the strategic influence of Personnel/HR is:

[Please tick ONE box only]

Very high						Very low
☐	☐	☐	☐	☐	☐	☐
1	2	3	4	5	6	7

6. Does your organisation recognise trade unions for the purposes of collective bargaining?

Yes	☐	1
No	☐	2
Don't know	☐	3

7. Does your organisation have a company pension scheme?

Yes		☐	1
No	} Go to Q9	☐	2
Don't know	} Go to Q9	☐	3

8. If YES to Q7, is this:

[Please tick ONE box only]

Contributory ☐ 1
Non-contributory ☐ 2

9. Would you describe the workforce at your SITE of WORK as:

[Please tick ONE box only in EACH column]

A		B	
Mostly male	☐ 1	Mostly young	☐ 1
Mostly female	☐ 2	Mostly mature	☐ 2
Equally divided	☐ 3	Equally divided	☐ 3

10. Would you describe the workforce in your ORGANISATION as:

[Please tick ONE box only in EACH column]

A		B	
Mostly male	☐ 1	Mostly young	☐ 1
Mostly female	☐ 2	Mostly mature	☐ 2
Equally divided	☐ 3	Equally divided	☐ 3

11. If you were to suggest an age for an "older employee" in your organisation, what might this be?

Years

a) For men: ....

b) For women: ....

12. In the LAST three years how far has the number of UK employees in your organisation increased or decreased?

[Please tick ONE box only]

Strongly increased			About the same			Strongly decreased
☐	☐	☐	☐	☐	☐	☐
1	2	3	4	5	6	7

13. How far do you think that the following may vary for your organisation in the NEXT three years?

[Please tick ONE box in EACH line]

	Strongly increased			About the same			Strongly decreased
Overall employment levels	☐	☐	☐	☐	☐	☐	☐
Task flexibility/ multi-skilling	☐	☐	☐	☐	☐	☐	☐
Proportion of older employees	☐	☐	☐	☐	☐	☐	☐
Ease of recruitment	☐	☐	☐	☐	☐	☐	☐
Availability of older people	☐	☐	☐	☐	☐	☐	☐
Recruitment of older people	☐	☐	☐	☐	☐	☐	☐
Job security	☐	☐	☐	☐	☐	☐	☐
Part-time working	☐	☐	☐	☐	☐	☐	☐
Work pressures	☐	☐	☐	☐	☐	☐	☐
Average workforce age	☐	☐	☐	☐	☐	☐	☐
Availability of younger people	☐	☐	☐	☐	☐	☐	☐
Recruitment of younger people	☐	☐	☐	☐	☐	☐	☐
Temporary/contract working	☐	☐	☐	☐	☐	☐	☐
	1	2	3	4	5	6	7

AGE AND EQUAL OPPORTUNITIES

---

14. Does your organisation have a written equal opportunities policy?

Yes	☐	1
No } Go to Q16	☐	2
Don't know } Go to Q16	☐	3

---

15. If YES to Q14, is age discrimination included?

Yes	☐	1
No	☐	2
Don't know	☐	3

---

16. Do managers usually receive equal opportunity training in your organisation?

Yes	☐	1
No	☐	2
Don't know	☐	3

---

17. Have you received any equal opportunities training in your organisation?

Yes	☐	1
No	☐	2

---

18. Have you received any equal opportunities training prior to your present organisation?

Yes	☐	1
No	☐	2

---

19. Do you think that employers should treat age as an equal opportunities issue?

Yes	☐	1
No } Go to Q21	☐	2
Don't know } Go to Q21	☐	3

5

20. If YES to Q19, how important is age compared to:

[Please tick ONE box in EACH line]

	More important	Equally important	Less important
Race	☐	☐	☐
Sex	☐	☐	☐
Disability	☐	☐	☐
	1	2	3

21. How far would you agree that age is relevant when considering employee....

[Please tick ONE box in EACH line]

	Strongly agree			Neither agree nor disagree			Strongly disagree
Recruitment	☐	☐	☐	☐	☐	☐	☐
Training	☐	☐	☐	☐	☐	☐	☐
Promotion	☐	☐	☐	☐	☐	☐	☐
Redundancy	☐	☐	☐	☐	☐	☐	☐
Retirement	☐	☐	☐	☐	☐	☐	☐
	1	2	3	4	5	6	7

22. Would you favour legislation:

a) to restrict the use of age limits in job advertisements?

Yes	☐	1
No	☐	2
Don't know	☐	3

b) in the form of comprehensive employment protection [comparable to race or sex legislation]?

Yes	☐	1
No	☐	2
Don't know	☐	3

6

23. How far would you agree that equal opportunity is:

[Please tick ONE box in EACH line]

	Strongly agree			Neither agree nor disagree			Strongly disagree
An important business issue	☐	☐	☐	☐	☐	☐	☐
Relevant to all employees	☐	☐	☐	☐	☐	☐	☐
A mainstream managerial activity	☐	☐	☐	☐	☐	☐	☐
An important moral issue	☐	☐	☐	☐	☐	☐	☐
Important for minority groups	☐	☐	☐	☐	☐	☐	☐
	1	2	3	4	5	6	7

24. The Department of Education and Employment is developing a campaign around age discrimination and 'older workers' in the UK. What age might you suggest as a general definition of an 'older worker'?

Years

a) For men: ....

b) For women: ....

7

POTENTIAL AGE BARRIERS

25. In your organisation, how far would you agree that because of their age older people would have less chance of being....

[Please tick ONE box in EACH line]

	Strongly agree			Neither agree nor disagree			Strongly disagree
Recruited	☐	☐	☐	☐	☐	☐	☐
Trained	☐	☐	☐	☐	☐	☐	☐
Promoted	☐	☐	☐	☐	☐	☐	☐
	1	2	3	4	5	6	7

26. In your organisation, how far would you agree that because of their age older people would have more chance of being....

	Strongly agree			Neither agree nor disagree			Strongly disagree
Made redundant	☐	☐	☐	☐	☐	☐	☐
	1	2	3	4	5	6	7

27. In your organisation, how far would you agree that older applicants would find it more difficult due to age to be recruited to....

[Please tick ONE box in EACH line - omit a line only where the occupational group is not applicable]

	Strongly agree			Neither agree nor disagree			Strongly disagree
Senior management	☐	☐	☐	☐	☐	☐	☐
Middle management	☐	☐	☐	☐	☐	☐	☐
Supervisory management	☐	☐	☐	☐	☐	☐	☐
Scientific/technical/ professional	☐	☐	☐	☐	☐	☐	☐
Clerical/administrative	☐	☐	☐	☐	☐	☐	☐
Skilled manual	☐	☐	☐	☐	☐	☐	☐
Unskilled manual	☐	☐	☐	☐	☐	☐	☐
	1	2	3	4	5	6	7

28. In recruitment and selection decisionmaking in your organisation, how far would you agree that....

[Please tick ONE box in EACH line]

	Strongly agree			Neither agree nor disagree			Strongly disagree
Procedures are highly formalised	☐	☐	☐	☐	☐	☐	☐
Age can be a formal criterion	☐	☐	☐	☐	☐	☐	☐
Age can be an informal criterion	☐	☐	☐	☐	☐	☐	☐
Age can be a justifiable consideration	☐	☐	☐	☐	☐	☐	☐
	1	2	3	4	5	6	7

29. How far would you agree that in your organisation the following could form potential obstacles to the recruitment of older people:

	Strongly agree			Neither agree not disagree			Strongly disagree
Limited recruitment activity	☐	☐	☐	☐	☐	☐	☐
Convenience of age as applicant filter	☐	☐	☐	☐	☐	☐	☐
Pension rules/costs	☐	☐	☐	☐	☐	☐	☐
Fixed retirement age	☐	☐	☐	☐	☐	☐	☐
Career/succession/ manpower planning	☐	☐	☐	☐	☐	☐	☐
Age of existing work teams	☐	☐	☐	☐	☐	☐	☐
Previous salaries of older applicants	☐	☐	☐	☐	☐	☐	☐
Customary recruitment patterns	☐	☐	☐	☐	☐	☐	☐
Jobs associated with certain ages	☐	☐	☐	☐	☐	☐	☐
Seniority pay/benefits systems	☐	☐	☐	☐	☐	☐	☐
Shortage of older applicants	☐	☐	☐	☐	☐	☐	☐
Customer expectations	☐	☐	☐	☐	☐	☐	☐
Focus on school leavers/ recent graduates	☐	☐	☐	☐	☐	☐	☐
Job demands/pace of change	☐	☐	☐	☐	☐	☐	☐
Interviewer age	☐	☐	☐	☐	☐	☐	☐
Trade unions							
Availability of younger people	☐	☐	☐	☐	☐	☐	☐
'Downsizing' focus on older employees	☐	☐	☐	☐	☐	☐	☐
Age stereotypes	☐	☐	☐	☐	☐	☐	☐
	1	2	3	4	5	6	7

RESTRUCTURING

30. In the last FIVE years, have efforts been made in your organisation to reduce the size of the workforce?

Yes	☐
No } Go to Q32	☐
Don't know } Go to Q32	☐

31. If YES to Q30, has a larger proportion of older employees been affected?

Yes	☐
No	☐
Don't know	☐

32. In the last FIVE years, have there been programmes in your organisation of:

	Yes	No	Don't know
Compulsory redundancies	☐	☐	☐
Voluntary redundancies	☐	☐	☐
Early retirements	☐	☐	☐
	1	2	3

33. Do you think that your organisation should focus on older employees as a means of reducing headcount?

Yes	☐	1
No	☐	2
Don't know	☐	3

34. The following have been suggested as advantages in focusing on older employees as a means of reducing headcount.

How far do you agree in relation to YOUR organisation?

[Please tick ONE box only in EACH line]

	Strongly agree			Neither agree nor disagree			Strongly disagree
Practical to operate	☐	☐	☐	☐	☐	☐	☐
Open up promotion channels	☐	☐	☐	☐	☐	☐	☐
Reduce wider workforce opposition	☐	☐	☐	☐	☐	☐	☐
Concentrate on most expensive employees	☐	☐	☐	☐	☐	☐	☐
Concentrate on less productive employees	☐	☐	☐	☐	☐	☐	☐
Reduce compulsory redundancies	☐	☐	☐	☐	☐	☐	☐
Meet aspirations for early retirement	☐	☐	☐	☐	☐	☐	☐
Can finance through pension funds	☐	☐	☐	☐	☐	☐	☐
	1	2	3	4	5	6	7

11

AGEING AND EMPLOYMENT CHARACTERISTICS

35. In general, how far would you say that the following may tend to increase or decrease with age?

[Please tick ONE box only in EACH line]

	Strongly increase			About the same			Strongly decrease
Reliability	☐	☐	☐	☐	☐	☐	☐
Pride in job	☐	☐	☐	☐	☐	☐	☐
Work speed	☐	☐	☐	☐	☐	☐	☐
Flexibility	☐	☐	☐	☐	☐	☐	☐
Physical ability	☐	☐	☐	☐	☐	☐	☐
Trainability	☐	☐	☐	☐	☐	☐	☐
Confidence	☐	☐	☐	☐	☐	☐	☐
Acceptance of authority	☐	☐	☐	☐	☐	☐	☐
Ambition	☐	☐	☐	☐	☐	☐	☐
Coping under pressure	☐	☐	☐	☐	☐	☐	☐
Teamwork abilities	☐	☐	☐	☐	☐	☐	☐
Responsibility	☐	☐	☐	☐	☐	☐	☐
Job satisfaction	☐	☐	☐	☐	☐	☐	☐
Loyalty to organisation	☐	☐	☐	☐	☐	☐	☐
Skills	☐	☐	☐	☐	☐	☐	☐
Insurance costs	☐	☐	☐	☐	☐	☐	☐
Benefit costs	☐	☐	☐	☐	☐	☐	☐
Short term absence	☐	☐	☐	☐	☐	☐	☐
Long term absence	☐	☐	☐	☐	☐	☐	☐
Turnover	☐	☐	☐	☐	☐	☐	☐
Energy	☐	☐	☐	☐	☐	☐	☐
Adaptability	☐	☐	☐	☐	☐	☐	☐
Qualifications	☐	☐	☐	☐	☐	☐	☐
Motivation	☐	☐	☐	☐	☐	☐	☐
Efficiency	☐	☐	☐	☐	☐	☐	☐
	1	2	3	4	5	6	7

36. In general, how far would you say that the following may tend to increase or decrease with age?

[Please tick ONE box only in EACH line]

	Strongly increase			About the same			Strongly decrease
Openness to technology	☐	☐	☐	☐	☐	☐	☐
Conscientiousness	☐	☐	☐	☐	☐	☐	☐
Performance	☐	☐	☐	☐	☐	☐	☐
Potential	☐	☐	☐	☐	☐	☐	☐
Ability to learn	☐	☐	☐	☐	☐	☐	☐
Customer service	☐	☐	☐	☐	☐	☐	☐
Productivity	☐	☐	☐	☐	☐	☐	☐
Work effort	☐	☐	☐	☐	☐	☐	☐
Wage costs	☐	☐	☐	☐	☐	☐	☐
Pension costs	☐	☐	☐	☐	☐	☐	☐
Accidents	☐	☐	☐	☐	☐	☐	☐
Sickness	☐	☐	☐	☐	☐	☐	☐
Commitment to quality	☐	☐	☐	☐	☐	☐	☐
Interest in training	☐	☐	☐	☐	☐	☐	☐
Quality of work	☐	☐	☐	☐	☐	☐	☐
	1	2	3	4	5	6	7

37. Please think now specifically about the workforce with which you are most familiar. How much might the following vary for older employees in comparison to others?

[Please tick ONE box only in EACH line]

	Much more			About the same			Much less
Work speed	☐	☐	☐	☐	☐	☐	☐
Openness to technology	☐	☐	☐	☐	☐	☐	☐
Absence	☐	☐	☐	☐	☐	☐	☐
Quality of work	☐	☐	☐	☐	☐	☐	☐
Flexibility	☐	☐	☐	☐	☐	☐	☐
Potential	☐	☐	☐	☐	☐	☐	☐
Ability to learn	☐	☐	☐	☐	☐	☐	☐
Work effort	☐	☐	☐	☐	☐	☐	☐
Employment costs	☐	☐	☐	☐	☐	☐	☐
Interest in training	☐	☐	☐	☐	☐	☐	☐
	1	2	3	4	5	6	7

13

INDIVIDUAL EXPERIENCE

38. Has age ever been a consideration in YOUR decisionmaking concerning employee....

	Yes	No	N/A
Recruitment/selection	☐	☐	☐
Promotion	☐	☐	☐
Training	☐	☐	☐
Redundancy/dismissal	☐	☐	☐
	1	2	3

39. Have you had any training in recruitment and selection techniques?

	Yes	No
a) In your organisation	☐	☐
b) Prior to your present organisation	☐	☐
	1	2

40. Within the last 12 months, about how much overall job related training/development have you received [if any]?

.... days

41. How would you rate this training on a scale of 1 - 10?

Very poor									Very good
☐	☐	☐	☐	☐	☐	☐	☐	☐	☐
1	2	3	4	5	6	7	8	9	10

42. Do you think that you have ever experienced any unfair disadvantage because of your relatively OLDER age in relation to:

	Yes	No	Don't know
A job application	☐	☐	☐
Promotion	☐	☐	☐
Training	☐	☐	☐
Appraisal	☐	☐	☐
Redundancy	☐	☐	☐
	1	2	3

14

43. Do you think that you have ever experienced any unfair disadvantage because of your relatively YOUNGER age in relation to:

	Yes	No	Don't know
A job application	☐	☐	☐
Promotion	☐	☐	☐
Training	☐	☐	☐
Appraisal	☐	☐	☐
Redundancy	☐	☐	☐
	1	2	3

YOU THE INDIVIDUAL

---

44. Are you:

Male	☐	1
Female	☐	2

---

45. How old are you?

Years

....

---

46. How long have you been with your current organisation?

0-2 years	☐	1
3-5	☐	2
6-10	☐	3
Over 10 years	☐	4

---

47. What is your management function?

[Please tick ONE box only]

Administration	☐	1
Production/engineering	☐	2
Computing/IT	☐	3
Management consultancy	☐	4
Purchasing/contracting	☐	5
Training	☐	6
Marketing/sales	☐	7
General management*	☐	8
Education	☐	9
R&D/design	☐	10
Finance	☐	11
Management services	☐	12
Distribution	☐	13
Personnel/HR/IR	☐	14
Corporate affairs/ PR	☐	15
Other *[Please specify]*..	☐	16

***Only tick this box if you have a senior role managing across functions**

16

48. What is your managerial level?

Board/chief executive	☐	1
Senior management	☐	2
Middle management	☐	3
Junior management	☐	4
Supervisory management	☐	5
Other *[Please specify]*..	☐	6

49. In which area do you a. live and b. work?

	Live	Work	
Northern Ireland	☐	☐	1
Scotland	☐	☐	2
North East	☐	☐	3
North West	☐	☐	4
Wales	☐	☐	5
West Midlands	☐	☐	6
East Midlands	☐	☐	7
East Anglia	☐	☐	8
South West	☐	☐	9
South East	☐	☐	10
London	☐	☐	11
Channel Islands	☐	☐	12

ANY OTHER COMMENTS

....

....

....

....

....

....

....

....

....

....

....

....

....

Thank you for your co-operation.

Your reply will be treated in strictest confidence.

Please return the questionnaire by **29th September 1995** in the reply-paid envelope provided to:

J Arrowsmith
Department of Management
The Manchester Metropolitan University
Aytoun Street
Manchester M1 3GH

18

Appendix 2 - Perceived association of age characteristics

Characteristics	Relationship with age						
	Strongly increase %			About the same %		Strongly decrease %	
	1	2	3	4	5	6	7
Reliability	18	37	28	1	2	1	1
Pride in jobs	14	34	28	20	3	1	1
Workspeed	1	6	15	40	33	4	1
Flexibility	4	8	16	26	36	9	2
Physical ability	0	2	6	22	53	14	2
Trainability	1	4	11	39	37	8	2
Confidence	11	29	34	17	8	1	0
Acceptance of authority	8	21	27	28	12	4	1
Ambition	1	4	13	29	38	13	3
Coping under pressure	6	19	30	28	13	4	1
Teamwork abilities	5	19	29	33	12	2	1
Responsibility	16	35	32	14	3	1	0
Job satisfaction	7	20	26	34	11	2	0

Loyalty to organisation	18	33	26	18	3	1	1
Skills	13	28	33	21	4	1	0
Insurance costs	3	11	24	54	6	1	0
Benefit costs	3	13	28	50	5	1	0
Short term absence	1	4	14	41	23	12	6
Long term absence	2	7	32	36	12	8	4
Turnover	1	4	8	29	24	24	10
Energy	0	3	9	40	41	7	1
Adaptabiltiy	1	6	17	28	39	9	1
Qualifications	3	14	27	35	13	6	1
Motivation	4	14	27	37	15	3	0
Efficiency	5	19	32	33	10	2	0
Openness to technology	0	2	9	26	45	15	3
Conscientiousness	8	27	40	21	2	0	0
Performance	3	13	33	41	10	1	0
Potential	1	5	18	39	31	5	1
Ability to learn	1	3	14	38	40	5	1
Customer Service	11	27	38	21	3	0	0
Productivity	3	10	31	43	13	1	0
Work effort	5	13	32	40	9	1	0
Wage costs	3	18	39	36	4	0	0
Pension costs	6	21	32	37	3	1	0
Accidents	0	20	10	59	20	7	1

Sickness	1	4	28	42	17	7	2
Commitment to quality	8	27	39	24	2	0	0
Interest in training	2	8	23	30	30	7	1
Quality of work	8	25	33	31	2	0	0

Appendix 3 - References

1 Arrowsmith J and McGoldrick A E [1994] Ageism in the Labour market: The Personnel Management Response *British Society of Gerontology Annual Conference* Royal Holloway, University of London, September

2 Taylor P and Walker A [1993] Employers and Older Workers *Employment* Gazette August pp371-378

3 Arrowsmith J and McGoldrick A E [1993] Recruitment Advertising : Discrimination on the Basis of Age *Employee Relations 15.5* pp 54-65

4 Thompson M [1991] *Last in the Queue ? Corporate Employment Policies and the Older Worker* Brighton, IMS

5 Itzin C and Phillipson C [1993] *Age Barriers at Work : Maximising the Potential of Mature and Older People,* Solihull: Metropolitan Authorities Recruitment Agency

6 Warr, P and Pennington J (1993). 'Views about Age Discrimination and older Workers' in *Age and Employment: Policies, Attitudes and Practices* London: Institute of Personnel Management

7 Arrowsmith J and McGoldrick A E (1995). Expectations of Labour Market and Developments, *British Academy of Management Annual Conference.* University of Sheffield, September

8 Leyens, J-P, Yzerbyt, V And Schadron, G (1994). *Stereotypes and Social Cognition London: Sage*

9 Benbow, N (1995) *Survival of the Fittest* London: Institute of Management

10 Private 'industry' is classified as those private sector cases which fall into categories 1-3 and 10-12 for question 2. Private 'services' are represented by 4-9 and 13-15. Of respondents working in the private sector, 55 per cent are located in industry and 45 per cent in services.

11 Items are listed in order of the strength of the correlation coefficient with the measure of perceived organisational recruitment discrimination against older workers (ie Question 25.1) rather than by frequency of agreement with the statement. This correlation provides an indicator of the explanatory power of the variable specifically in relation to age discriminatory practices. For example, the highest level of simple agreement is with the statement that 'limited recruitment activity' acts as a barrier to the employment of older workers. However, this is not one of the highest correlates (ie is a less powerful potential preditor) of perceived age discrimination, since it necessarily serves to include individuals of all age groups from the organisation. Accordingly, it occupies a position lower down the table.

All the correlations are statistically significant at the p<.001 level, except for the final two which are not statistically significant.

12 Arrowsmith, J and McGoldrick A E (1994) The Future resourcing of the service sector: in C Armistead (ed) *The future of Services Management* Cranfield School of Management/Kogan Page pp 131-151.

13 Worsley, R (1996) Only prejudices are old and tired; *People Management,* January p18-20

14 Theoretical understanding is therefore under-developed. Age discrimination may, however, be characterised as a demand-side process which is related *objectively* to certain organisational structural conditions and change processes, and *subjectively* to the operationalisation of stereotypical views of the supply side of the labour market. Organisational *and* individual characteristics are therefore be simultaneously the appropriate focus of study. A large body of theoretical work may therefore be relevant: life cycle and career theories fromdevelopmental and organisational psychology; segmentation and human capital theory from labour market economics and dependency

and stigmatisation theory from sociology. Ongoing analyses of the data are testing the relative contributions of this work. The application of regression and path analytic techniques is also being used to construct alternative models of age discrimination in order to generate further theoretical understanding.

Other recent IM Reports

Other research reports published by the Institute of Management are listed on the following pages. For further information, or to order, please contact:

The Representation Unit
The Institute of Management
3rd Floor
2 Savoy Court
Strand
London WC2R 0EZ

Tel: 0171 497 0580
Fax: 0171 497 0463

Back to the Line?

A survey of managers' attitudes to human resource management issues

Professor Michael Poole &
Glenville Jenkins

The development of an organisation's key resources - its employees - is probably the biggest responsibility and challenge facing British managers. In the uncertain climate created by recession and technological change, human resource issues are moving more to the forefront of organisational policy making.

The aims of the survey were to investigate:

- how human resource departments are organised
- the changing role of human resource management
- how and where responsibility is shared between traditional personnel departments and line management
- experience of employee involvement, training and development initiatives and various work and reward practices

The report concludes that the link between human resource management and sustained competitive advantage is likely to become stronger and more important in the latter part of the 20th century.

£25.00 IM Members and Subscribing Organisations
£50.00 Non Members

ISBN: 0-85946-254-4

February 1996

Survival of the Fittest

A survey of managers' experiences of, and attitudes to, work in the post recession economy

Neville Benbow

Managers are increasingly being required to demonstrate flexibility and adaptability in their approach to work. Job security is no longer an accepted norm and with the trend towards portfolio careers, what kind of person is the post recession UK manager? Have career/financial expectations changed with economic recovery and in what way?

The aims of the survey were to investigate:

- the impact of the 1990s recession on managers
- attitudes to future career development
- extent of career path changes
- attitudes to financial security

The report provides practical recommendations to act as a checklist for individuals in ensuring their employability. Organisations will also benefit from advice aimed at providing an environment which is conducive to effective working and learning.

£25.00 IM Members and Subscribing Organisations
£50.00 Non Members

ISBN: 0-85946-253-6

November 1995

Striking off the Shackles

A survey of managers' attitudes to employee involvement

Mark Fenton-O'Creevy

Much has been written in recent years about the benefits and problems of employee involvement and empowerment which is defined as the direct involvement of employees in making decisions about how their work is carried out. In the right circumstances these practices can deliver considerable benefits such as increased job satisfaction, improved productivity and greater success in managing people.

Little attention has been paid however to the opinion of managers who are often expected to implement such programmes.

The aims of the survey therefore were to investigate:

- desired versus actual extent of employee involvement
- views about its value and benefits
- the relationship with managerial empowerment

The report enables the reader to benchmark employee involvement in his or her own organisation and also provides practical recommendations for effective implementation.

£25.00 IM Members and Subscribing Organisations
£50.00 Non Members

ISBN: 0-85946-252-8

September 1995